THREE AND TWO!

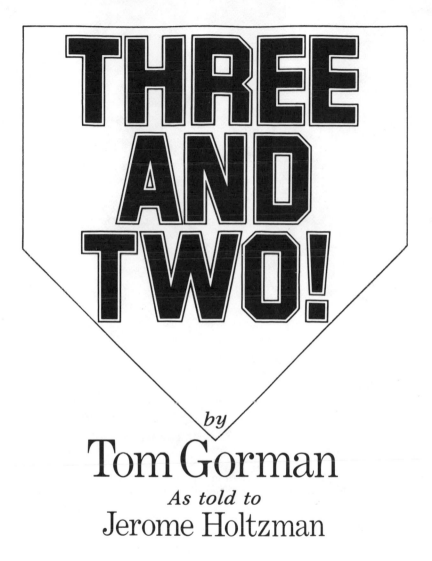

by

Tom Gorman

As told to

Jerome Holtzman

Charles Scribner's Sons [] *New York*

3 5 7 9 11 13 15 17 19 H/C 20 18 16 14 12 10 8 6 4 2

Printed in the United States of America
Library of Congress Catalog Card Number 79-84382
ISBN 0-684-16169-9

To my wife
Margie
and to my four children
Tommy, Patty Ellen, Kevin, and Brian

THREE AND TWO!

1

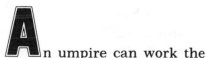

n umpire can work the plate in a pitcher's perfect game, and nobody's going to come up and shake his hand. I know. I saw it happen. I was there, working the left-field line in Yankee Stadium in 1956 when Don Larsen pitched the only perfect game in World Series history. Twenty-seven batters, twenty-seven consecutive outs. And you probably can't remember the name of the umpire who worked the plate.

Babe Pinelli, a good umpire, a very good umpire, worked the plate on that day, his last plate game. He retired two days later. Babe Pinelli was the Lou Gehrig of the umpires, our Iron Man. Twenty-two years in the National League, never missed a game. He was the forgotten man on Larsen's big day.

Pinelli called it all the way, down to a tough decision on Larsen's last pitch. With two outs in the ninth, Dale Mitchell came in as a pinch batter for the Dodgers. The first pitch was a ball. Mitchell then took a strike and swung and missed, for strike two. Larsen's next pitch was on the outside corner.

"Strike three," Pinelli shouted, and the perfect game was in the books. Some sportswriters and players later said the last pitch was outside, that it should have been a ball. There are still arguments about it. But that was in the future.

The crowd—more than sixty thousand people—jumped to its feet. Yogi Berra, the Yankee catcher, ran to the mound and leaped. Larsen caught him like a baby. They made one of the famous pictures in baseball history: Larsen holding Yogi in his arms. The Yankee players and the fans cheered and jumped up and down. They almost knocked Larsen flat with congratulations. As they should have done. It was a perfect game, a rare and astonishing accomplishment under any circumstances, absolutely stunning in a World Series. A small group of men—six of us, the umpires, in dark blue suits—walked off the field, ignored and forgotten. We went into our dressing room. It was empty. Babe Pinelli cried like a baby.

Not one person came in to congratulate Pinelli, to say, "Babe, you did a fine job—twenty-two years in the league and you finish with the first perfect game in World Series history."

Nobody showed, not the commissioner, not the president of the National League. I thought it was a disgrace.

But let's say that Pinelli had called that last pitch to Mitchell a ball. The count goes to two and two. And let's say Mitchell hits the next pitch for a home run, or between short and third for a single. That's the end of Larsen's perfect game. From then on anything is possible.

But history never reveals its alternatives. I don't know what would have happened on the playing field. But I do know if Pinelli's call on Mitchell had broken up Larsen's perfect game, it would have become a thing of ferocious interest. You wouldn't have been able to get into our dressing room. The Yankee players would have been screaming. The sportswriters would have come on Pinelli in waves, like the Marines on a beachhead. "Babe, why didn't you call it a strike?" "Wasn't it a strike?" "Are you sure?" "But Yogi said it was a strike. He said it caught the corner."

And so it would have gone. But that's the way we play our game. If everything is easy, every call a natural, you don't see anybody. If there's trouble you see everybody. We know that. We accept it, just as we accept the lonely travel; the dreary years in the minors; the long months on the road away from our families; the abuse from the players, the managers, and the sportswriters. Sometimes we wish our lives were different. But we know they aren't different and never will be.

This is a book about umpires in general and one umpire in particular—how we became umpires, what it takes to become an umpire, why we stick with it. I stuck with it because I loved it. This book will tell you why.

To begin my life at the beginning, I was born in Hell's Kitchen, between Ninth and Tenth avenues, on the West Side of New York, on March 16, 1919, an hour before St. Patrick's Day. The name of the place was worse than the place itself. Hell's Kitchen was, in fact, very nice, as I remember it. It was a mixed neighborhood; there were kids to play with, schools and churches to attend, and homes to return to when you'd tire of playing in the streets. And there were those streets—I know that kids accustomed to parks and playgrounds wouldn't have taken to them, but more often than not we had nowhere else to go.

And so, as kids have always done, we did with what we had. We played stickball mostly, using sewer covers for bases. We never knew we were "disadvantaged" or "poor" or "deprived" or "victims of society." We were not. We had advantages. We had food on the table and clothes on our backs, and parents who cared. What more does a kid need?

My family was as Irish as you can get. Both my grandparents came from Ireland. The name my father's father brought with him was O'Gorman, but somewhere the *O* got lost, as most Irish *O*'s did in America. Grandfather and Grandmother came from County Cork, or somewhere thereabouts—Francis O'Gorman, looking for bread and work in the New World. He was a cop—so were my father and one of his brothers—and he fell off a roof one night, chasing a prowler. The fall killed him. He was only forty-seven—an age that seems younger every year I get older. He had three sons: my father, Dave, the oldest; Tom, the other cop; and Vinnie, who worked for the telephone company.

My mother's name was Katherine Moran, the daughter of emigrants from County Mayo, I believe. Someday I'd like to go back to Ireland and find out—and about my father's people, too. I called my mother Kate, never Mom or Mother. She was a good woman—she looked after us—and a great cook. There were thousands of Irish families just like ours, but we didn't think about that, or realize it. To ourselves we were special, unique, a little world. I think all of us felt that way—Mother, Father, my older sister Helen, who lives in Yonkers now, and Mary, who lives in Jackson Heights, and myself, the only boy. It was a home where a child could grow up knowing he was loved, knowing he would be taken care of, knowing if he did wrong he would be punished—a good Irish family, Roman Catholic, that went to mass every Sunday, respected the priests and nuns —without really liking some of them—and never got into serious trouble. The Irish in our neighborhood had strict schools that taught you right from wrong. The Irish Christian Brothers used to carry a strap about an inch wide and take a shot at us now and then. If I went home and told my father I'd been hit, he'd say, "You must have done something wrong."

We respected authority. If you were hanging out on a corner and a cop came along and said, "Hey, get going," you'd better get going. If my father said anything, we'd better do it. It was a rule in our household that we come home at night when the lights were turned on in the streets. We couldn't claim we were unable to find a clock or a watch. The lights came on, home we'd go. My father never hit us—he only spoke to us, and if we'd committed an offense that he thought was particularly bad, he'd keep us in all day. There was no worse punishment than not being allowed to go out and play.

Wherever we lived—in Hell's Kitchen, Far Rockaway, the Bronx, not far from the Polo Grounds and Yankee Stadium, the East Side in a sixth-floor apartment at 747 East 168th Street, the big thing in my life was sports, particularly baseball and basketball. Basketball occupied a big place in my early life. The big, successful teams, the ones I like to remember, were at Power Memorial High School. This is the school that Kareem Abdul Jabbar came out of many years later. He broke most of the school records that I made when I was at Power. My height was good for center—six-two, six-two-and-a-half—and we had a great coach, an Irish Christian Brother named Louftous. Brother Louftous brought the zone defense into New York and was the first one to coach it in high school. It was a fast league—the Catholic League that included teams in all five boroughs of New York City. Without that league to play in, and without the coaching of Brother Louftous, I wouldn't have been able to play pro basketball later in life, as I did for thirteen years.

As a professional basketball player, before and after

World War II, I moved about among teams in the Pennsylvania State Pro League and the New York State Pro League, and I played half a year in the National Basketball Association, for Toronto. Then I returned to the New York League to become playing manager at Glens Falls. Kate Smith had a club in that league, Smith's Celtics. I had two jobs for a couple of years during that time—with Glens Falls, and with Rice High School, as basketball coach. In New York City the pro teams played at the old Hippodrome—twice a week, a Saturday-night game and one during the week. The crowds were small by today's standards —a thousand, eleven hundred, twelve hundred. Compared with today's basketball it was nothing, but we made a living, we played our best, we had a good time. Sometimes I wonder if the present-day game is as enjoyable, with its crowds, its money, its endorsements, its pressures. I don't know, but I do remember my playing days with great pleasure and satisfaction.

But more important than *that* career was the other, baseball, which eventually became my life's work. When I was a kid we had one good suit—our Sunday suit—and we put it on for Sunday mass and for visits with the relatives, and then we took it off and put on old pants and shirts for our afternoon of stickball and baseball. For stickball I'd steal my mother's broom and take off the wires and the straw. She used to have nice brooms, and she always wondered what became of them. Once I rewound the wire around the straw, so that it looked as if it hadn't been tampered with, and returned it to its place, but when she tried to use it the wire unwound and the straw fell apart and my mother was completely puzzled and angered. She was going to return the broom to the store and raise hell with the clerk for selling her such poor merchandise, but I couldn't let her be embarrassed that way. I confessed all. She could have killed me. Brooms weren't our only problem. Sometimes the cops would chase us because the neighbors complained, and we'd hide the sticks in the sewer and take them out when the cops left.

But, as Saint Paul wrote, when I became a man I put away childish things. Stickball became a memory, and I became a very good baseball pitcher. At Power I had an athletic scholarship, for baseball *and* basketball, and I pitched two years when we won the city championship, in 1936 and 1937. My father encouraged me as much as he could. Being a New York cop—one of New York's finest— was his life, and he spent thirty-five years on the force. For thirty-two years he was on the same beat—traffic, at Forty-third Street and Fifth Avenue. But when he could he had always joined me in baseball. In fact, he had played a little semipro ball himself. Dave Francis Gorman, the cop— always working, four to twelve, eight to four, midnight to eight, but still a good father. In the streets we played with taped balls and bats, and what mitts and gloves we could find. My father once gave me a glove. Somebody gave him a twenty-five-dollar gift certificate for Christmas, just before I got out of high school, and when he told me it was good at a sporting goods store, I asked him if he would buy me a glove. He thought a glove wouldn't cost much, five or six dollars, but a good glove even in those days came to about eighteen dollars. Today it'd be sixty dollars. He may have been surprised by the price, but I had my glove, the first good one I ever owned: a left-handed pitcher's glove with short fingers, called the Carl Hubbell Model. That was the only thing in all the world that I wanted for that Christmas. I've still got it.

My father did even more. On Sundays, when he could, he took me to see the Yankees, to watch Lou Gehrig and Babe Ruth. Gehrig was my hero. It was a sad day when he retired, when we learned he was going to die. It just didn't seem right, such a great man, such a good physical specimen.

Gehrig was a good one, all right, and I met him once—

a big moment in my life. He raised and showed German Shepherds and we kids used to pick up some extra money by working at the armory at 168th Street and Fulton Avenue. We'd walk the polo ponies or take care of the dogs. And once at a dog show, who should walk in but Lou Gehrig and his two German Shepherds. I got his dogs to take care of—to wash, brush, and walk, and to guard just by sitting in front of the cages. We didn't say much to each other, Gehrig and I—just a question or two, a yes or a no. He gave me five dollars. But the money aside, it was *the* big time of my young life. Kids need heroes; they need heroes in sports, in education, in politics; they need *good* heroes. Hell, adults need good heroes, too.

Even more than the Yankees, my father's heroes were the New York Giants. He began taking me to Giant games on Sunday afternoons when I was no more than six or seven years old. His particular hero was first baseman Bill Terry, a great hitter—he had a .341 lifetime average—who later managed the Giants. It was my good fortune to bring them together on one occasion. It'll take a little time to tell how. In 1937, before I had graduated from high school and I'd been offered basketball and baseball scholarships at a couple of colleges, but my real interest was in getting into professional ball. Pancho Snyder and I had been going to the Polo Grounds to pitch batting practice for the Giants, and it turned out that the Giants wanted to sign me. Even though my father had taken me most often to the Giants games, I'd been more of a Yankee fan as a kid, because of Lou Gehrig and Babe Ruth and because I lived in the Bronx. But across the river were the Giants and they wanted me to play for them!

Bill Terry told me this one afternoon and I went home knowing I'd have to tell my father. I was a minor—eighteen years of age—and he'd have to sign for me. He got home about five o'clock and I didn't wait. "Tomorrow you've got to go down to the Polo Grounds," I said. "The Giants want to sign me."

He looked at me for a moment. I suppose he had to let the news sink in. I've never seen a man so amazed. He hadn't even known I was pitching batting practice for the Giants. "What do you mean, the Giants?" he said. I told him about the batting practice. He thought I was kidding. I told him again he'd have to go to the Polo Grounds and sign for me. But he said he had to work the next morning. "Well," I said, "Bill Terry would like to see you tomorrow morning around ten, ten thirty."

"Bill Terry?" he said. "Bill Terry?" "Yes," I said, "Bill Terry himself."

"Did you tell your mother?" he asked me. "Yes," I said, "I mentioned it to Kate." I don't think he believed it, even after several minutes, but he called the station and got the day off.

And so here he was, face to face with Bill Terry, with the possibility that his son was about to go to work for him, about to play for the Giants he had loved all those years. Terry gave my father a cigar—my father kept it, unsmoked, to the end of his days—and before getting down to business they talked about what a fine boy I was, what a good specimen of an athlete. They agreed I had a good chance, I had a good fastball; but Bill Terry and the Giants could teach me a lot. It'd take a couple of years—they'd have to send me to a farm club—but then I ought to be a very valuable baseball property. They knew I had a chance to go to college but that I didn't want that; I wanted to play pro ball. They thought it was a wise choice. And my father said to Bill Terry, "I admired watching you play all these years. You were a great ballplayer, and you're a great manager. I've been a Giant fan for a long time."

"Well," Terry said, "I'm glad you like the Giants. It's nice to see a Giant rooter. A lot of people don't like me in this business because I'm a hard man, but I'm a good man and I always try to be fair. We want to be fair with you. That's why you're here. You have to sign for him, and we wouldn't want to do anything without your consent. Now, it's up to you. What do you want to do?"

"Can I talk to Tom for a minute?" my father asked. Terry nodded, and he took me outside. "Do you want to do this?" he asked me. "I'll do what you want me to do. Do you want to play ball, or do you want to go to school?" I told him I wanted to play ball. "Okay," he said, and we went back into the office. "Mr. Terry"—I remember now that every time my father spoke to him, it was never Bill; it was always Mr. Terry—"Mr. Terry," he said, "we'll sign."

Suddenly I was a professional baseball player.

I know my father was more amazed than I was. And he never understood the bonus they gave me. Bonuses were just beginning in baseball at that time. They were more a gift than anything else, to help you get to whatever minor-league city they were sending you to. Mine was five hundred dollars.

"Why should they give you five hundred dollars just for signing a piece of paper?" my father asked. I couldn't explain it myself, but I took the money. It was all the money in the world to me then. From nothing to five hundred dollars with the stroke of a pen; from high school to the big leagues.

My father and I went home happy and dazzled. He saw me pitch for the Giants once, at the Polo Grounds, at the end of the 1940 season. He never saw me umpire in the big leagues. He died in 1945.

o, playing basketball in the off-season, I was now a professional baseball player. I think you have to be one to know what being one is like. You've heard about all the great players all your life—you'll remember I even met Gehrig once—and you've picked out your heroes and villains, your favorite teams, the teams you dislike, for whatever reason, and suddenly you're where you thought you'd never be, ready to join that great beautiful world out there on the playing field, to actually play ball before a paying crowd, and get paid to play. At that moment it would seem like a bargain if you played for nothing—even if you had to pay for the privilege. I went home from Bill Terry's office without really knowing how I got home. I suppose I floated. My father was pleased too, of course, and still puzzled. "You mean they give you five hundred dollars for doing nothing," he said again. "Just for signing a paper?" He shook his head in disbelief. "I never knew baseball was so generous."

But eventually you come down to earth—to the dirt, sand, lime, and grass where the game is played—and you do what they tell you. After I signed, I pitched batting practice for the Giants and finished my schoolwork. I didn't play ball my senior year in high school because I had signed a professional contract.

My first stop in professional baseball was Blytheville, Arkansas, a Giants farm team called, appropriately, the Giants of the Northeast Arkansas League. This was Class D, the lowest you could get in professional baseball. *These* Giants carried three starting pitchers and one relief pitcher. And all of these minor-league games called for only two umpires, a fact I didn't especially notice until later.

Hershel Bobo, who worked for the New York Giants, was the manager at Blytheville. We had a good ball club. Along came June and we were in the middle of a pennant race. I was supposed to go back to New York to get my high school diploma, but if I left for a few days I'd throw the pitching rotation off and maybe hurt our chances. Bobo told me he'd let me go but said he'd like to see me stay. He talked to Bill Terry, who said they'd have to let me go if I wanted to. "But if you can talk him out of it, okay." Bobo didn't have to talk too hard. I wanted to win as much as he did. So the night of the graduation ceremonies my father picked up my diploma, on the stage at Town Hall, and the school principal announced that I was away on business. Everybody knew I was playing ball.

I won fifteen games at Blytheville and lost only nine, not bad for a young kid, a wild left-hander, breaking into pro ball. The Giants were impressed, but what they really noticed was my ratio of strikeouts for innings pitched. I wasn't Sandy Koufax, but I did have 166 strikeouts in 198 innings. And like Koufax, I was wild. I gave up 100 walks. It was the only time in my career that I led a league—and on two counts. I had the most strikeouts. But I also had the most walks.

The ball park was in the middle of a racetrack. The clubhouse was nothing. We had no lockers, just nails on the wall. Everybody took a turn driving the team bus. There was no meal money. Once in a while they'd take us into a diner and buy us a couple of hamburgers.

My salary was one hundred dollars a month, and I was one of the highest paid players on the team. Stan Musial was breaking in at the same time and he got sixty-five dollars a month. Money wasn't the object. The big thing was to get to the big leagues.

The Giants then promoted me to Class B, to Clinton, Iowa, in the Three Eye League. The Clinton manager was Blondy Ryan. Some old-time fans still remember him. He had been a player with the Giants, a weak hitter, a .239 lifetime average. At one point during his playing career he had been out with a spike wound and was getting ready to rejoin the Giants, who were in St. Louis for a crucial series with the Cardinals. He sent a telegram to Bill Terry:

AM ON MY WAY. THEY CAN'T BEAT US.

Later, Blondy said he hadn't meant that the two sentences in his telegram had any connection with each other. Terry showed the telegram to the sportswriters and Blondy Ryan became a footnote in baseball history. That wire gave the Giants the psychological lift they needed. The other players picked up the rallying cry, "They Can't Beat Us," and the Giants rolled on to win the National League pennant.

From time to time, Ryan would call for the knockdown

pitch. I never believed in hurting anybody, but the knock-down pitch was and still is a part of baseball. You push the hitter back off the plate. If the same guy got two hits in a row off you, Blondy would give the knockdown sign and the next time the hitter went down. You didn't throw at his head. You pitched inside to him, to get him off the plate. Bill Terry managed the same way. Terry would flash the knockdown sign and if the pitcher didn't knock the hitter down Terry would fine him ten dollars. In those days ten dollars was a lot of money. Most of the guys would knock their mother down for ten dollars.

I was no angel, but I never got into trouble with the umpires. I used to argue once in a while. If you don't argue, you're not human. But I was never ejected. I only remember two umpires from the Three Eye League. I think their names were Ruff and Tuff. They worked together, good umpires. My roommate at that time was a kid named Red Sheehan, an outfielder from New Haven, Connecticut. He got as far as Jersey City, Class A. He drove a truck in the off-season and got killed in an accident. It was a rotten shame.

Clinton was a good town for the players. They had a diner where you paid five dollars for a card and you could eat for a week. My record in Clinton was only 7–8, but I must have shown some promise, because they promoted me to Jersey City. And I was in Jersey City for only about ten days before the Giants brought me up. I was thrilled. I still hadn't completed two full years in the minors and I was on my way to the Polo Grounds and baseball glory.

I thought I was ready, that I could handle big-league hitters. I guess Terry thought so too. I was young, in wonderful condition, and eager to work. The Giants had Carl Hubbell, Cliff Melton, and Bill Lohrman, and they were getting along in age. The club was trying to bring up some young players to take their places. They also brought up Harry Feldman, Rube Fischer, and Steve Tramback, young pitchers like myself, all of us with bright futures. We never thought about World War II. The old-timers helped me, Hubbell most of all. He was coming to the end of his great career and he helped this wild boy from the Bronx.

But I was a rookie, and they treated me like one. I wore a new fifteen-dollar pair of shoes into the clubhouse one day and the veterans spit tobacco juice on them, and laughed like hell. They'd soak a hot rubbing ointment into my jockstrap, and wait for my pain and surprise. They nailed my shoes to the floor.

One day Willie Schaffer, the old trainer with the Giants, got me in trouble with Bill Terry. It was near the end of the season; just a few games were left on the schedule. I was very eager. I wanted more than anything else to start a game. So I asked Schaffer. "I wonder," I said. "We've only got three or four games left. Do you think Mr. Terry would let me start a game?"

"Why don't you go in and ask him?"

"Do you think it'd be all right?"

"Sure. Go ahead. Ask him."

Terry came in at about ten o'clock. I was ready for him. I knocked on his door and said, "Mr. Terry, can I see you for a minute?"

"Sure, what's on your mind? Is anything wrong?"

"No," I said, "but I was wondering if it would be all right for me to start a game?"

I didn't realize the sin I had committed. "Who the hell is the manager of this club?" he roared. "You just came up. You're a busher. And don't ever forget it. I'll start you when I want to. Now get your ass out of here."

He was a hard man, but fair, and he always encouraged me. "We'll bring you along slowly," he said. "You're going to be a damn good pitcher."

As it turned out, I pitched only five innings in the big leagues, all at the end of the '39 season. I had one tough moment. Terry put me in relief in a game against the Cardinals. Bases loaded and Joe Medwick, one of the toughest hitters in the league, was at bat. I got two quick strikes on him and then tried to fool him with a change-up. He hit it into the seats. I just stood there and watched the ball. He hit the damn thing so far I thought it would never come down. But I learned. Never throw a change-up to Joe Medwick. I learned other things, too. How to field my position, how to mix up my pitches.

I was back at Jersey City in the International League in 1940 and the next spring, 1941, I was back with the Giants. Terry was using me in a lot of the Grapefruit League games and things were looking good. Then I got a call from home. It was my mother. The draft board wanted to know where I was. A few days later they sent a telegram. Report immediately. Terry helped me pack my bag.

I drove home. My father was retired by then and I could have claimed my parents as dependents. I was supporting them. But I didn't want a deferment. I decided to enlist for a year. Then I'd be out the following March, just in time for spring training. You remember the song that came out about then, "Good-bye dear, I'll be back in a year." So we thought. The war broke out in December. I didn't come back for four years.

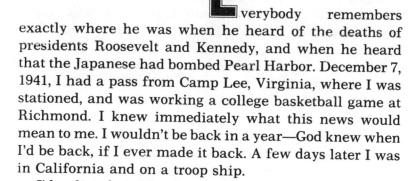

Everybody remembers exactly where he was when he heard of the deaths of presidents Roosevelt and Kennedy, and when he heard that the Japanese had bombed Pearl Harbor. December 7, 1941, I had a pass from Camp Lee, Virginia, where I was stationed, and was working a college basketball game at Richmond. I knew immediately what this news would mean to me. I wouldn't be back in a year—God knew when I'd be back, if I ever made it back. A few days later I was in California and on a troop ship.

I'd enlisted on March 6, 1941, and been sent to Camp Dix, New Jersey (now Fort Dix). I suppose I wandered about as much as any GI—from Dix to Fort Meade, Virginia; to Camp Stoneham, near San Diego; to the Middle East for several stops; and then home. It all seems random and accidental now, but I suppose that there was a plan for it, somewhere, that'd make sense of it.

In the army nobody asked me to play baseball—and this was to have a decisive effect upon my baseball career when I was released. I was a foot soldier. I carried a Springfield rifle. I was a GI, a footslogger, a dogface—in the Sixteenth Infantry of the First Division. Like millions of others. I have no complaints. I made sergeant finally, and just before the Italian invasion got to within about thirty miles of the front. Near Tripoli one day, I was riding in the back seat of a jeep. The driver and another passenger were in the front seat. We ran over a field mine—a bouncing beauty, they called it. Somebody, it seemed to me, had taken hold of that jeep and thrown it straight up in the air. The driver was killed. When I came to, I was flat on my back on a stretcher in an ambulance, beginning to feel pain. I'd been hit in my right shinbone, just below the knee. I stayed in the military hospital at Cairo for six weeks.

Everybody knows that it is, after all, a small world: while I was recuperating I met a chaplain major named Father Carey, who had been athletic director at Seton Hall and had wanted to give me a basketball scholarship. I told him I'd signed with the Giants. He asked me if I wanted to organize some sports in Cairo. I was glad to; it would give me something to do, both civilian and athletic. We citizen soldiers never quite forgot, I suppose, that we were civilians. So I organized service teams in baseball, football, and basketball. My leg was still gimpy, and they sent me home in January 1945 and set me completely free in October 1945, shortly after the war with Japan ended. I had an uncertain future. During my last weeks in uniform I was in the hospital at Atlantic City, waiting for my discharge. On the night of September 17, 1945, my father went out to get a package of cigarettes. He dropped dead of a heart attack in a candy store. I remember it was a Friday night. I couldn't get home. I was in the hospital awaiting reassignment.

I returned from the war and took a wife, as many of us veterans did. Margie and I had lived in the same New York neighborhood. She used to hang out with my sisters and we'd all go out dancing together. We didn't really consider those evenings dates. The popular dance at the time was the Big Apple, and we'd go to the big hotels where the big bands got started—Glenn Miller, Harry James, Tommy Dorsey. I remembered Margie through the whole war, and we corresponded some. It was when I returned that I had my first real dates with her. I took her out dancing, and to a couple of ball games.

I proposed to her at one of those games. The Giants were playing Cincinnati in the Polo Grounds, and they won four to two. I remember the pitcher who got the win —Harold Henry Schumacher, Prince Hal—who was approaching the end of his career. In the fourth or fifth inning I turned to Margie and said, "You know, we've been going together for a while. Why don't we get married?"

She looked at me in surprise. She didn't think I was serious. She laughed and said, "You get married?"

I got angry. Why not me? People *did* get married. Stranger things had happened. I gave her a ring, and we were married in October 1945.

There's probably one question they won't ask you if you want to be an umpire: What kind of wife do you have? Yet it's an important question. An umpire's wife—like a baseball player's wife—has got to be patient and long-suffering. She's home alone for months at a time. She has the full responsibility for the children during those long separations. She shouldn't complain too much, and she should love her husband and sports in about equal amounts. Margie did love sports—hockey, basketball, and baseball—and she was a fine bowler.

I never remember a time when she said, "Let's go to a movie instead of a ball game." When I was on the road and called home, she always asked how the game was going, how the teams were doing. Sometimes she'd join me for weekends when I was in the International League. Once she was sitting in the stands near a fan who was yelling at me—terrible things, threats, curses, accusations. She hit him with her pocketbook. She almost opened his skull. They gave her a cheer. All our kids like sports, too. How could they help it?

In the spring of 1946 I reported to the Giants at Winter Haven, Florida, for spring training. I was out of the army, I had a new wife, and it soon developed I also had a sore shoulder. The years of inactivity in the army had taken their toll. I had developed a deposit of calcium just where it would hurt a left-handed pitcher most. This became the worst-kept secret of my life. How can a pitcher make a secret of arm trouble? Maybe he can shoot in the novocaine, but that doesn't last forever. Sometimes nothing in the world can help. I don't know whether the Giants knew or suspected my trouble, but they did trade me to the Boston Braves, and I joined the Braves at Fort Lauderdale. This was a change, but nothing compared with what was coming.

My wife joined me at Fort Lauderdale, and I went through my workouts. I knew enough to know I was in trouble. Yet I pitched pretty well. One afternoon I went seven innings against the Giants and shut them out. Somebody must have been watching, because that night a scout for the Pasquels, the big baseball boys in Mexico, came to the Brown Hotel and made me an offer. I was impressed and excited. Maybe this was my way to hang on for a while. It turned out it was a way for me to make more money than I'd make with the Braves or any other American team. Billy Southworth, manager of the Braves, had said enough to indicate he was doubtful of my future.

"The way you're throwing right now," he'd told me, "well, maybe your arm will come around. You're still young. You've got a chance. Maybe we'll send you to the Eastern League."

I wanted no more minor-league ball. I wanted to play in the majors and I needed money. The Mexican scout told me he was speaking for one of the Pasquel brothers, Bernardo. They would give me an $8,000 bonus and $12,000 a year for three years. That'd be $20,000 immediately, $24,-000 more eventually—a total of $44,000. That was real wealth in 1946, especially to a broke ex-soldier, to a pitcher with a sore shoulder, to anybody I'd ever known.

So I went back to see Billy Southworth. "Billy," I said, "I've got an offer to go to Mexico. I've got a chance to make some money. But I want to be honest with you because I'm not going to jump the ball club. I want to talk to you first."

"Do you want to go?" he asked.

"Yes, Billy, I want to go. I need this type of money. If I go to Mexico and if I can throw pretty good in the hot weather there, I can always come back."

"I'll tell you what, Tom," he said, and he did me the biggest favor anybody's ever done for me. "I'm going to give you your release, but don't tell anybody about it."

Everybody thought I had jumped the ball club, but I believe I was the only player who went south of the border who wasn't a jumper. Even Muddy Ruel, who at that time was the assistant to the commissioner, thought I had jumped, and when I came back he got on my case. But my departure was perfectly legal.

The other players, because they didn't get releases, were regarded as outlaws and were not allowed to play in the States for five years. That's what Billy Southworth did for me.

Margie and I had $218 between us, and we needed a ride to Mexico. In a Miami paper we found an ad placed by a man who wanted somebody to share the costs of a trip to Mexico. His name was Max Posen, a Russian Jew, a good guy who dealt in jewelry and hats. I went to see him and told him we wanted to go to Laredo, Texas, where we were to be met by a representative of the Pasquels. Max Posen said he wasn't going that direction. I told him it was a big emergency. We had to get there; we didn't have money for a train or a plane. We sat down and talked money, and left the next morning. He drove a while, I drove a while, all the way to the Palace Hotel in Laredo. The car stopped right there. It wouldn't go another inch. We had burned out the clutch. But we had made it, all the way to another league, in another country.

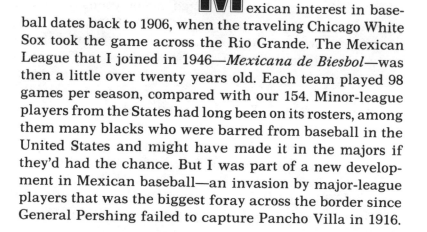

Mexican interest in baseball dates back to 1906, when the traveling Chicago White Sox took the game across the Rio Grande. The Mexican League that I joined in 1946—*Mexicana de Biesbol*—was then a little over twenty years old. Each team played 98 games per season, compared with our 154. Minor-league players from the States had long been on its rosters, among them many blacks who were barred from baseball in the United States and might have made it in the majors if they'd had the chance. But I was part of a new development in Mexican baseball—an invasion by major-league players that was the biggest foray across the border since General Pershing failed to capture Pancho Villa in 1916.

This new invasion, however, was organized and financed by the Mexicans themselves, specifically by a remarkable family of five brothers named Pasquel. The Pasquels had inherited a large fortune and several profitable businesses from their father. They were the official customs officers for most of Mexico's imports and also had investments in real estate, newspapers, cattle, cigar manufacture, and the construction business. They were the friends and supporters of presidents. And they owned the Mexican League.

The head of the clan was Jorge Pasquel, president and executive chairman of the league, owner and president of the Veracruz team, and builder and operator of Delta Park, in Mexico City, the home field not only for Mexico City but for Veracruz as well—to the disgust of many loyal Veracruz fans. Though part of his fortune came from tobacco, he hated smoking and his office contained large signs forbidding it. On the floor of his office lay the pelt of a gray mountain lion that he had shot himself—complete with head and big teeth. They called it Ted Williams. When Jorge talked with visitors, he often placed a .45 automatic pistol on his desk, within easy reach.

Jorge was about forty in 1946. His brother Bernardo, who was a little older, was the diplomat, the foreign secretary of the clan. He conducted negotiations with the American players. Next came the twins, Gerardo and Alfonso, who were a little over thirty. They confined themselves largely to the family's other businesses. The youngest, Mario, was in his mid-twenties. He met the stars from the United States and put them on a train to Mexico City.

But it was Jorge who originated the raids on the majors, who directed them and provided their financing. He was a genuine patriot, a Mexican chauvinist. The people he hurt were the major-league moguls, but his real target, I suspect, was the entire United States of America. Like many another people, the Mexicans love to see a little man defeat a big man—or a mere human being dispatch a tremendous bull. Jorge managed to assemble twenty or more American major-league ballplayers for the eight teams in his league. A few of them were virtual rookies like me, with dubious futures. But most of them were known to every fan in the States. Here were Lou Klein, Max Lanier, and Fred Martin from the St. Louis Cardinals; Sal Maglie, Danny Gardella, Nap Reyes, Roy Zimmerman, and George Hausmann from the New York Giants; Rene Monteagudo from Philadelphia; Vern Stephens and Ray Hayworth from the St. Louis Browns; Alex Carrasquel from the Senators; Mickey Owen and Luis Olmo from the Dodgers; and yours truly, a sore-armed left-handed pitcher from the Boston Braves. A pretty fair collection of catchers, fielders, and pitchers.

Not all of the enticements succeeded. The Pasquels failed to capture such players as Ted Williams, Bob Feller, and Stan Musial. And the Pasquels had problems with some of their American stars. Vern Stephens, who had led the American League in home runs in 1945, quit the Mexican League and returned to the Browns after a couple of games. Stephens refunded his salary advance, but not all of the American players did when they quit early. Mickey Owen, the Giant catcher, was, allegedly, among them. The Pasquels sued Owen, and Owen responded by suing the Pasquels. Don't ask me who won. Later, Danny Gardella sued the major leagues to force them to lift the ban on players who had jumped. He didn't think he was an outlaw and, I guess, legally he wasn't. The big-league owners gave him a secret $300,000 settlement. Gardella and some of the other jumpers did sit out for two or three years, but almost all of them finished their careers in the major leagues.

When I arrived in Laredo Bernardo Pasquel, the ambassador brother, met me at the Palace, the only hotel on the American side of town. He told me his brother Jorge wanted to see me in Mexico City. They had a plane waiting. Margie was exhausted by the trip and had gone to bed.

[25]

I got her up and off we flew to Mexico City. When we got there, the Pasquels made me feel like Babe Ruth. A Cadillac met us at the airport. And before Bernardo took us to see his brother he drove us to the ball park. A game was in progress. Danny Gardella, Roy Zimmerman, Mickey Owen were there, among the first wave of players to come from the States. I was escorted onto the field between innings. The field announcer introduced me and I took a bow. They hadn't even seen me pitch and already they were cheering me.

Then we drove, in the same style and comfort, to Jorge Pasquel's office. It was a large, elaborate office with that warning against smoking. Jorge greeted me, sat down, and wrote out the contract.

"I agree," I said, feeling like a bridegroom saying *I do.*

"How do you want to be paid?"

"In cash."

He opened a drawer of his desk and took out a wad of bills, most of them thousands. He counted off $20,000 and laid it out on the desk—as he had promised. There was an $8,000 bonus and $12,000 in salary for the first year. I later learned the white American players were paid on an average of about twice what the Latins and American blacks were paid. Mickey Owen, for instance, signed for $15,000 a year, plus living expenses that included a free apartment, and Mrs. Owen was promised a diamond ring for helping persuade her husband to play in Mexico. Most of the Americans had exactly the same motive—to make some money and get out. We were on velvet. I thought I was. Twenty thousand was more money than I'd ever had before, and more than I was to have for a long time in the future. And there it was, right there before me on the desk, waiting for me to pick it up. Jorge put all that money into a paper sack, a little grocery bag, and handed it to me. So I had twenty grand and hadn't thrown a ball. And I still didn't know what team I was going to play for.

Jorge Pasquel told me, "Now you're going back to Laredo. It's on the border. You can live in Texas or Mexico."

"If it's okay with you," I said, "I'll live in Texas."

It was all right with him so long as I played for the half of Laredo that was on the Mexican side. I put the money in a small attaché case. I was terrified I'd lose the money, or somebody would steal it. Money, I was learning, had its curses. It wouldn't let you sleep.

Jorge Pasquel took Margie and me to dinner that night, and then to the jai alai games, and we flew back to Laredo the next day.

Max Posen, who had furnished our transportation from Florida, came around the next morning. He had read about me in the paper and wanted to know why I hadn't told him. He was a baseball fan. I asked him what happened to the car and he told me about the burned-out clutch. I gave him some money to have it fixed, and haven't seen him since.

The town, I learned, was divided by the Rio Grande, but it wasn't grand at this point—a small, creek-sized stream, crossed by a small bridge. The Laredo stadium had no dressing rooms. I would put on my uniform at the hotel. The team manager, a man named Garcia, told me they played on Sundays, Wednesdays, Thursdays, and Saturdays. My day would be Sunday. There were eight teams in the league: Mexico City, Veracruz, Tampico, Puebla, Torreón, San Luis Potosí, Monterrey, and Laredo. Mexico City had the only decent accommodations. There was little or no provision for dressing and showering. They were all skin infields. But, for the money, I could take it—for a while.

I asked Garcia how many other Americans were on the Laredo team. I was the only one. I always knew how the blacks felt when they first got to the big leagues and when there were only one or two black players on every team. It was lonesome, but we got along all right. We traveled together, played together, and talked and joked together, and made a team. Our travel and hotel reservations were made by the club. Sometimes, crossing the hot, flat, dry country by train, I saw the hovels that some of the people called home, and I began to realize why so many of the Latins played good ball. Everyplace, even the poorest of villages, had its players. Every kid in town, it seemed, played baseball with homemade bats and balls. It wasn't all that much different from Hell's Kitchen in New York. Perhaps baseball is one of the things that makes the whole world kin, or at least the Western Hemisphere and Japan.

The crowds in Mexico, though small by our standards, were noisy and demonstrative. There were few women in the stands, but there were always a lot of lottery vendors, who sold lottery tickets and acted as bookies. The Mexican fans would bet on everything, whether the next pitch would be a ball or strike, or even if the batter would hit a foul ball. Most of the stands had no aisles and the fans had to climb over each other to get to their seats.

And that wasn't the only inconvenience. One afternoon in Alijadores Park, in Tampico, the plate umpire, a wonderful man named Maestri, a short man who wore elevator shoes, suddenly called time. I couldn't figure out why he'd stopped the game, but then a door opened in left field and out came a train—a real choo-choo train—pulling a string of oil cars. It crossed the field about twenty feet behind second base and went out through a door in the right-field fence. This was in the fourth inning. In the eighth inning the right-field door opened and another train came puffing through. And then it was on with the game!

As for my pitching, I was in good physical shape, but after four or five innings I could feel the effects of the calcium. Once I got warmed up and was throwing, it was all right. But when I sat down between innings, it was hard for me to crank up again. There just wasn't enough fluid going through the arm. I won my first game 5–2, but in the late innings my arm was killing me. I needed help. I sought out Wayne Black, the fellow who ran the Palace Hotel.

"Wayne," I said, "do you know any doctor in town, somebody who could work on my arm? I need help."

Wayne said there was a regular doctor in town, a bona fide M.D., a good guy. I went to him.

He examined my shoulder and arm and asked if I'd ever used novocaine.

"I've used different things," I said. "But never novocaine."

"It'll help your pitching," he told me. "But if you get immune to it, it's tough. You can use it once a week. Come here after mass on Sunday morning. I'll shoot you about an hour before the game. We'll see how it works."

Novocaine doesn't heal. It's only a painkiller and athletes who use it risk further harm to an already crippled joint. But what I wanted, and what most athletes want, was immediate relief, without regard to the consequences, and that's what I got.

In my second game, after the doctor had shot me, I was unbeatable. I was Walter Johnson, Lefty Grove, and Sandy Koufax rolled into one. I could have thrown the ball through a wall. "Oh, boy, this is great," I said to myself. "What a snap." I won the game easily and next time out I pitched a two-hit shutout. But after that game I woke up at four o'clock the next morning: I was in agony. I had to walk the streets for two hours. I couldn't lie or sit. Margie told me I was crazy. I was risking my whole future. But I wanted to play. I paid the doctor's fare to go on the road with us. The novocaine worked well for four or five hours. Then the effects would wear off. It was like having a massive toothache—in the shoulder.

I lost my fourth game but won the fifth. I was 4–1, not

bad. But the next Sunday the doctor was called out of town on an emergency. I had to pitch without help. I worked five good innings and was winning 3–1. But when I came out for the sixth I couldn't throw the ball to the plate. Manager Garcia asked me what was wrong. I told him I must have pulled a muscle. The next day there was a big story saying that Tom Gorman, the American southpaw, had hurt his arm. Garcia took me to the team doctor and the doctor said the same thing I had said: a pulled muscle. There was no mention of calcium, or the possibility that I was using novocaine.

Somehow—I don't know how—I got through the season. I pitched every Sunday except two, when we were rained out. I had a 7–3 record. The other players had good years, too. The sluggers could get more distance because of the rarefied air. In Mexico, the altitude goes up seventy-five hundred feet above sea level. But because of the thin air you tire more easily than in the States, and while the pitchers could throw a faster fastball, their curves didn't have as good a break. And now and then one of us would come down with the *turistas,* Montezuma's revenge, they called it! And it was some revenge!

Eventually you get adjusted to the thin air and to the drinking water, but there were other things that Margie and I couldn't adjust to. The Mexican people seemed to be very jealous of the Americans. I guess they had good reason to look at us with envy. Our life-style was a lot better than theirs. Life seemed very cheap down there.

One night I saw Bernardo kill a guy. He just pulled out a gun and shot him and that was that. There was a cocktail party in Bernardo's backyard and this guy was climbing over the fence. I don't know what the hell he wanted. But Bernardo shot a hole in him as big as a cucumber and everybody walked away and left him lying there as if it was a perfectly natural thing.

Jorge Pasquel brought us back in January 1947, and we

had a meeting in Mexico City, a dozen or so American players and some of the owners of the Mexican clubs. Bernardo Pasquel then told us that his brothers had lost a barrelful of money the season before. Our contracts were cut in half and now we had to pay our own expenses. Of course nobody liked what they did. I would get only $6,000 for the second year. They gave me a $2,000 advance. I felt I was wasting my time. And my shoulder was worse. I made two starts, lost them both, and decided it was time to get out. I didn't know what I would do. Because of the release Billy Southworth had given me, I wasn't an outlaw. But I knew I'd never pitch again.

One fine day I left, without saying good-bye to anybody.

In the winter of 1947 I was back in New York, out of a job, almost broke, and with no idea of what I could do. Margie, who had not gone with me to Mexico for the second season, was working as a secretary at IBM, but I couldn't let her support me. I began coaching and playing professional basketball and officiating, but at small pay. I didn't even try to return to baseball. I wouldn't have made it in Class D.

One night I was working a game between St. John's and Holy Cross at Madison Square Garden and the chief scout for the Boston Red Sox, Neil Mahoney, came to see me in the dressing room. Neil asked me what I was going to do. I told him I didn't know.

Neil then told me he could get me one of two jobs. He could get me a spot as a manager for one of the Red Sox farm teams, or as an umpire in the New England League. The minor-league managing job didn't surprise me. Horace Stoneham, the owner of the Giants, had made me the same offer but I had turned it down. I didn't think I was cut out to manage.

When Neil mentioned the possibility of me being an umpire I thought he was off his rocker.

"Now, don't get mad at me," Neil said. "I think you'd make a good umpire. You've got the right kind of temperament and you've got good size. You know baseball. You've been around."

"You're out of your mind. You'd get me killed out there. Me umpire? Forget it!"

Neil gave me his card. "Let me know," he said. "Claude B. Davidson, up in the New England League in Boston, needs four umpires."

I'd turned him down, but the idea stuck with me. The more I thought about it, the more I liked it. I called Neil and told him I might be interested.

"All right, good," he said. "Meet me Sunday in New Haven. Claude Davidson will be there, the president of the New England League. They're having a league meeting."

"Sunday," I said. "I've got a game Sunday."

"Well, this is more important than the game."

"Yes, sure, but the game pays fifty bucks. That's a lot of money." But I said all right, and promised to meet him.

Neil was waiting for me in the lobby of the New Haven Hotel. "I'm going to take you up to meet Davidson," he said. "If he asks you any questions about umpiring tell him you've umpired."

I'd never umpired in my life, and I told Neil so.

"But tell him you umpired. You've been around baseball long enough. I know he's going to offer you a job."

I met Claude Davidson—a big man, bluff and hearty.

He asked me if I'd like to umpire professionally.

"Yes, I think I would," I said. "I've been in baseball a couple of years and I've done a lot of officiating in the army."

"Well," he said, "we've got a couple of openings. We'd like to have you. You've got good size. We'll have another umpire meeting and go over everything."

Nobody had mentioned money. "Mr. Davidson," I said, "what does it pay?"

"Our league pays good," he said. "A hundred and eighty dollars a month."

I repeated the amount after him—a hundred and eighty dollars a month.

"By the way, Tom," he asked, "have you got a car?"

I told him I did.

"You've got a car, you've got a job," he said.

So if I hadn't had a car, I wouldn't have had a job.

"But, Mr. Davidson," I said, "one eighty a month isn't a hell of a lot."

"That's how it is," he said. "You might get sixty dollars a month for expenses, but we don't know yet. I'll be in touch with you."

We left, and downstairs I told Neil I could make more than one eighty selling newspapers. "And if I'm umpiring," I said, "I have to have a room, I have to go out to eat. How're you going to make it on one eighty a month?"

"Tom," Neil said patiently, "they all start like this."

"And I have to get a suit and shoes, and protectors. I'd be working for nothing. Forget it."

I went home and told Marge. "Let's forget it," I said. "A guy offered me one eighty a month. And if I didn't have a car, I didn't have a job. It's more important to have a car than to know anything about umpiring."

"Do what you want," she said.

I didn't know what to do.

About a week later I got a contract in the mail: one

eighty a month, plus fifty-five dollars a month expenses.

"Why don't you try it," Marge said. "Try it for a year."

"All right," I said. "You want me to, I'll try it."

And so I began a new career.

I started the season with a guy named Dave Clary as my partner. I didn't know it then, but he would turn out to be a great guy. From Brockton, Massachusetts, the home of Rocky Marciano. Jim Duffy and Hank Soar, both of whom later worked in the American League, were in the New England League at that time, too. They were partners, big buddies from Pawtucket, Rhode Island. Like Dave, they were veterans and had been umpiring for a couple of years.

Dave and I had our first game in Nashua, New Hampshire. Walter Alston was the manager at Nashua then. I knew some of the players—Don Newcombe, Roy Campanella, Joe Black, all of whom later made it big with the Brooklyn Dodgers.

Dave was going to work the plate and I was going to be on the bases. On the drive to Nashua, Dave started telling me the different positions to take according to the circumstances: where to position myself with a man on first base, a man on second, and so on. Then he says, "Where did you umpire last?"

Well, I want to be honest with the guy I'm umpiring with, so I tell him.

"Dave," I said, "I'll tell you the truth. I've never umpired a game in my life."

He almost ran the car off the road.

He pulled over to the side and said, "Tommy, what do you mean?"

I said, "I've never umpired a game in my life."

"How the hell did you get the job?"

"Mr. Davidson offered it to me and I took it. I've played on a lot of ball fields, but I've never umpired."

"You've never called balls and strikes?"

"Never."

He was thinking I was going to get him killed. There's only two of us. There aren't four.

Finally he said, "I have to give you credit. You got a lot of balls."

But while he was giving me credit, I knew what he was thinking: This is a B league and the umpiring is pretty tough.

We went to the park, got dressed, and walked onto the field. It was one of those games where nothing happened —what we call an open game. Everything was safe and out. No close plays. No conflict.

On the way home I said, "This ain't too bad."

"Yeah," he says, "we did all right. It was an easy game. But tomorrow night you've got to go behind the plate. And you've got to get into the hole, in the chute and everything else."

I said, "Yeah, well, I've watched umpires. I think I can do it."

The next night who is pitching but Don Newcombe. He can really throw that ball. I didn't have a peep. Boom, boom. Everything was quiet. Both sides.

We stopped at a diner on the way home, and Dave looked at me and he said, "You sure you never umpired before?"

"Never."

"You're doing a helluva job."

It was in Pawtucket, Rhode Island, that I had my first rhubarb. George Kissell, who later was a coach with the St. Louis Cardinals, was the manager. I called the tying run out at the plate in extra innings, the eleventh or twelfth. I thought it was a hell of a call. But Kissell didn't, and all hell broke loose. We had a real hassle and I had to unload him. He was the first one to go, number one on my ejection list.

One night Dave got sick and a guy named Jack Brady

filled in. Jack worked in the navy yard and was used in emergencies. That night Jack and I had a game between Lynn, Massachusetts, and Manchester, New Hampshire. Tommy LaSorda, who now manages the Los Angeles Dodgers, was a pitcher on that Manchester club.

Jack worked the bases and had three close plays, all in a row. The first one was a play at second, which I thought he called right. Then another banger, this one at first base, and then another close play at second. They all went against the same club, Lynn.

The Lynn manager was steaming. He came out and he and Jack got into a tussle. Then one of the Lynn players called Jack a sonofabitch and—*whack!*—Jack hit the player right between the horns. Brady hit him first, no doubt about it.

By the time I got Jack out of there, they had torn the coat off my back. Everybody got into it. My first real brawl. When it was over, not only was my coat gone but my shirt and undershirt were torn. From the waist up, I was almost naked. All I had left was my chest protector. We had to get the police to escort us out of the ball park after the game.

The first thing I did when I got back to the rooming house was to call Davidson. He already knew what had happened. He said to me, "I understand Brady hit one of the ballplayers first."

I said, "That's right, he did hit him, but the guy isn't used to being called those kind of names and he let him have it."

Then I said, "You know, Mr. Davidson, during the tussle they tore the coat off my back."

He laughed like hell.

"How am I going to get a new one?"

"That's up to you."

I said, "Well, I've only got one uniform and I'm umpiring tomorrow."

"You'll have to get one someplace," Davidson said. "Get

[*37*]

it patched up. Do something. That's part of the game."

And that's how I broke in. The more I umpired, the more I liked it. I finished the season with life and limb intact, and I went back the next year. Halfway into my second season Davidson sold me to the International League and in 1950 the National League bought me. Many people don't realize that umpires are "bought" and "sold" by the league just as players are by the team. But I didn't come up to the National League until 1951, the year the league went from a three- to a four-man system.

ll umpires remember
their first major-league game. It's like the first time you
make love. You never forget. My first game was in Chicago, at Wrigley Field, on September 9, 1951.

I made my debut at third base and broke in with three
very good umpires, three of the best—Al Barlick, Lee Ballanfant, and Augie Donatelli. I made one mistake. A batter
hit a pop fly near the Cub dugout and the third baseman
made the catch on a slab of concrete next to the bat rack.
I yelled, "No catch." In the International League, concrete
was not part of the playing field. Ballanfant was working
second. He hurried over and corrected me. "We allow that
in this league," he said.

The next day I had the plate. Bill Lee pitched for the Cubs and pitched a low-hit game, a very good game. I don't remember the other pitcher. But I do recall that after the game Lee stopped me as I was going through the dugout runway and he said, "Hey, kid. Good game." It was a big thrill to me then. I didn't think they said those things in the big leagues.

From Chicago we went to the Polo Grounds in New York, and that's when I met Leo the Lip. He was managing the Giants. I had a play at second base and he comes running out and says, "Hey, kid, I want to tell you something. You called the play too quick."

"He's out and that's the way it's going to be. And don't call me kid."

"Oh, tough guy," he said. "You're going to be like the rest of 'em."

I told him I didn't know about the other umpires, but that his man was out.

Leo started walking away, back to the dugout. He took five or six steps and then made sort of a half-turn and let me have it. He called me a sonofabitch. But he didn't do it to my face so there was nothing I could do about it.

A week later we were in Brooklyn, and we had the Giants again. I was working first base. Another close play. And, of course, I heard the roar of the crowd and the patter of Durocher's little feet. I waited. I let him get closer. Then, when he was about five feet away, I said, "Get out of the game! Get the hell out of here!"

"But, Tom, I haven't said anything."

"I know. But that's for the last game in the Polo Grounds. Now we're even."

That was my first ejection. I don't remember who was number two. Maybe it was Leo again. He was a beaut. There were times, in my first few years, when I'd get up in the middle of the night and I'd see him coming out of the dugout. You could always count on seeing him when there was a sellout crowd, or if the game was on national television. He was an actor. He should have been on the stage. He'd throw his arms up and yell and carry on against an umpire and the fans loved it.

A lot of it was for show. Once, in Brooklyn, he went jaw to jaw with Al Barlick. The fans thought it was wonderful. When the rhubarb was over Leo walked away but accidentally stepped on Barlick's foot. Barlick was a tough guy, a great umpire.

After stepping on Barlick's foot, Leo said, "Gee, Al, I'm sorry." And Leo meant it. I'm sure he was afraid of Barlick.

But the fans roared again, thinking Leo was getting one final shot at Barlick when all he was doing was apologizing.

I didn't throw out a lot of guys. Before I retired, somebody in the National League office made up a list of the umpires and their total ejections. I was near the bottom. I had fifty-five or fifty-six, no more than two to three a season. My last one was Ron Cey of the Dodgers. I called him out on a third strike. He didn't like it and threw his bat toward my feet. So I unloaded him.

Sometimes you can go for a whole year without throwing anybody out. Billy Williams and I had a year like that. Very peaceful. Or you can go for a month without hearing a peep. Then the next two, three days, you're in the middle of the Johnstown flood. Nothing but trouble.

It was like that with me and Durocher. We had our ups and downs. It wasn't one continual argument. There were months of peace. But he always wanted the edge in everything. He kept everybody on edge, not only the umpires but his players, too.

We got a new National League president in 1970. Chub Feeney succeeded Warren Giles, and Chub got this bright idea. In the last week or two of spring training he sent out a letter, a very beautiful letter, to all the umpires, and in it he said, "On opening day I want each umpire to shake hands with each manager and wish him luck."

Now, I knew what Chubby was trying to do. He was trying to improve our public relations. He was also crazy: most of the umpires don't talk to half the managers in the league.

I read this nice let's-get-friendly letter and then checked my schedule. I opened in Chicago with the Cubs and Phillies. Just my luck. I'd get Durocher and Gene Mauch.

So I called San Francisco, league headquarters.

"Chubby, this is Tom Gorman."

He said, "Tom, I knew you'd call."

And I said, "I'm not going to shake hands with nobody —especially Durocher and Mauch. I don't even talk to those guys."

"Well, you're going to talk to them now and wish them luck, or it's going to cost you three hundred dollars."

"Three hundred bucks? Well, for three hundred bucks I'd shake hands with the devil."

So I got to Chicago. Beautiful day. Ferguson Jenkins was pitching. Good pitcher. Out came Gene Mauch. Now, I hadn't talked to this guy in two years. "Hello, Gene," I said, "nice to see you. The best of luck for the rest of the season."

He looked at me and said, "What the hell is the matter with you? I didn't know you could talk, and now you're wishing me luck. It's amazing."

We had a full house, thirty-nine thousand people. After everyone was seated, Durocher came out, an actor on center stage. Like a good soldier I carried out my duty. I gritted my teeth and said, "Hello, Leo, it's nice to see you. The best of luck for the rest of the season."

Do you know what he said to me?

"Horseshit."

He marched back to the dugout.

I said to myself, "Some way, somehow, I've got to get a

piece of him today." Jenkins pitched a strong game and won 3–2. I didn't have a pitch or a play at the plate that could bait Durocher out of the dugout. Once in a while we bait them out. Once you've got them on the green, you have a shot at them.

The next day I was at third base. Nothing happened. The following day I was working second base. Again, nothing happened. The final game of the series I was at first base and got a bang-bang—extremely close—play. As soon as it happened, I said to myself, "Thank God for the play."

Don Kessinger of the Cubs had hit a slow roller and I called him out at first base. It was like opening the door. Out came Durocher. In Chicago the home dugout is behind third base. He had to come all the way across the field to get me. Leo was now in his sixties. He couldn't run too good. I backed up. You always make them come a little further. When he caught up to me, I was halfway into right field and he was screaming, hollering, "Hey, Tom? Hey, Tom! How in the world can you call that man out?"

The veins were coming up his neck. His eyeballs were popping.

I said to myself, "Let him holler a little longer. Maybe he'll have a heart attack."

Finally I said, "Leo, what are you hollering about?"

"How the hell can Kessinger be out?"

"Leo, he tagged the base with the wrong foot."

He stopped and looked at me, like I was a nut. He didn't know what to say. I had him stumped. He had a bewildered look on his face, like he forgot what he was arguing about. He turned around and walked away. When he got back to the dugout, I could see him talking to some of his players. I could tell they didn't know what he was talking about.

The game ended an hour later. Our dressing room was behind the Cub dugout and he was in the runway waiting for me. As I came in, he said, "Hey, Tom, I want to talk to you."

"What is it, Leo?"

"How long have you been in this league?"

"Twenty years."

He said, "I want to tell you something, Tom, and I'm only going to tell you once. They can tag first base with any foot."

Three months later, on July 5, I was back in Chicago. I remember the date. It was the day I broke my leg, one of my several injuries during thirty years of umpiring. The Cubs were playing the Pittsburgh Pirates. I was working first base, my unlucky position.

Al Oliver was playing first for the Pirates and Dock Ellis was pitching. Paul Popovich was the batter and he hit one down to first base, about twenty feet to the right side of the bag. Oliver moved over to field the ball. All Ellis had to do is run from the mound to first to cover. Simple play. Popovich is out by twenty to twenty-five feet.

But Ellis forgot to cover. He's on the mound picking his nose, or counting his money. I don't know what the hell he was doing. Here comes Popovich down the line and here comes Oliver, running like hell back to first base. I said, "Oh, oh, we're going to have a nice bang-banger here." I went to the outside, in foul territory. You always go to the outside of the play. I got down on one knee, good position, to make the call.

Popovich and Oliver got to the bag at the same time. There was an awful crash. Tremendous collision. Before I could make a call, Oliver was thrown into me. His head hit me in the pit of the stomach. I thought my whole body had fallen apart. I was on the ground with the wind knocked out of me, trying to catch my breath. Trying like hell. And the next thing I heard was, "Did he call him out, or did he call him safe?"

It was Durocher talking to Danny Murtaugh, the Pittsburgh manager.

I'm lying there half dead. I didn't know it then, but my leg was broken. I said to myself, "Tom, get up off the ground."

I'm still struggling. Again I hear this voice: "Was he safe? Or was he out?"

So I say, "Who's talking?"

He says, "It's me. Leo."

I say, "Well, if it's Leo, he's out."

Then they carried me off the field and took me to the hospital. The next day Durocher was the first guy to come and see me. Nine o'clock in the morning, and he was there, asking me if I needed anything. On the field and off the field, he's two different men.

Once Leo and I made a television commercial for Gillette. We met at a Chicago studio, at seven in the morning. I said, "Hello, Hook, how are you?"

He said, pleading, "Please don't call me Hook. Not today. These people won't understand."

A lot of umpires called him Hook, because of that big schnozz of his.

"Tom, let's be friends for this one day."

I said, "Okay, Hook," and we went in and signed releases and then went to see the makeup man. We got the works. Pancake makeup. Eyebrow pencil. Hair dye. It was like going to the beauty shop. It took more than an hour. When he got out of his chair I said to him, "C'mon over, Hook. You look so beautiful, I want to kiss you."

The commercial ran thirty seconds, but it took us eight hours to make it. We kept forgetting our lines. We had a lot of fun and made a good piece of change out of it. It was supposed to run for a year and a half, and the longer it ran, the more money we'd make. We got ninety-seven dollars every time it got on, the best deal I've ever had. It was on for about two months, but then the Cubs fired

Durocher and it went down the drain. I could've killed him.

Leo had open-heart surgery a couple of years ago. My daughter, Patty Ellen, saw it in the paper and told me about it. He was in Houston. Just like Leo to have Dr. DeBakey open him up.

Leo always went to the top. I remember once he was telling some sportswriters that someday he would do his autobiography, but that he was sorry Ernie couldn't do it.

"Ernie who?" they asked.

"Ernie Hemingway," Leo replied.

I didn't know how to get hold of Leo in Houston. He always has a private number. So I called his friend in New York, Murray Saklad, the dentist. Even when he lived in Chicago and Los Angeles, Leo always went to New York to get his teeth fixed.

Dr. Saklad gave me the number. A nurse at the Houston hospital answered. I told her I was one of the umpires in the National League, that Mr. Durocher was an old friend of mine. I was calling to see how he was doing. She said he was downstairs getting X rays, or something. Maybe they were giving him a bath. The next day he called me.

He said, "Gee, Tom, I can't get over you calling me. Of all people to call me. Makes me feel very delighted. Not many people have called me."

I said, "I know."

He kind of giggled at that.

"Tom," he said. "The troubles we've had. You've chased me out of so many games. The fights. The arguments. I never expected you to call me. It's unbelievable. I told everybody at the hospital about you. This really pleases me. Let me ask you something, Tom. Why did you call me?"

"Leo," I said, "I wanted to see if you were dying."

Leo's in kind of a shell now, holed up out there in Palm Springs, California, though I understand he did make a few appearances promoting the 1978 All-Star game. But he doesn't go out like he used to. I had a chance to do one of those light beer commercials with him, but he didn't want to come to New York.

I know he wasn't always a nice guy. He was tough on reporters and he was tough on umpires. But all in all, he was good for baseball. You just had to know how to handle him. When he'd come out to get a piece of a young umpire I'd always hover, like a mother hen. He'd say, "Tom, it's not your argument. Leave us alone." But I'd say, "Oh, no, I'm in this, too. I want to hear what you've got to say."

Then he'd have to come at me. It was a good strategy and it worked. Once he said, "Tom, my argument's at second base and here I am arguing with you."

I said, "Leo, you go over there and I'm going to unload you."

"Goddamnit, Tom, you know all the tricks, don't you."

And I'd tell him, "I sure do. I had a lot of good teachers being around guys like you."

The biggest thing about umpiring, above all, is control—control of the game. An umpire can't get mad. You must be patient and slow to anger. Once you lose your head you lose everything. Sometimes you've got to grit your teeth. When the language gets rough, you unload 'em. Always remember, the umpire doesn't have the last word, he has the last two words: "Get out!"

Every time there is an ejection or an unusual occurrence, the crew chief must write a report to the league office. We're not sportswriters, but sometimes you'd think we were. Those reports can be lengthy. The league wants details. They also want your recommendation: one-day suspension, two days, three days, five days. If you suggest a player be fined, how much? Nowadays a player, if fined or suspended, can ask for a hearing. He can file an appeal. It's one of the rights the players won through their Players Association.

An umpire shouldn't play the tough guy. We're not Humphrey Bogart or Jimmy Cagney or Edward G. Robinson. In our game you can't be a patsy either, but you've got to allow the managers to have their say. You don't want them to stand there and read you the Congressional Record, but they're entitled to a few sentences.

Billy Williams, my partner for eleven years, had a quick temper when he first came up. Mr. Giles was worried about him. He put Billy with me. Mr. Giles said, "Calm him down and tell him to get rid of those rabbit ears." An umpire with "rabbit ears" reacts to everything that's said, even if it's said almost in a whisper. It's a real disadvantage to have rabbit ears. But I'm happy to say Billy calmed down, and he's become one of the best umpires in the major leagues.

The next thing an umpire must learn is timing. You should never hurry your call, or anticipate the play. If you're quick with the trigger, you've got an easier chance of being wrong. You wait for the play to be completed. If you hold your call and take another look—and if you have good position—you're going to be right 99 percent of the time, maybe more. When an umpire kicks a play, it's usually because he was too quick with his call. I always told my younger umpires, "Take your time. That extra half-second will make life a lot easier."

We rotate around the diamond according to seniority. In the World Series, for example, the senior man opens behind the plate, the second senior man works first base, then second base, third base, and so on. In the Series we have two extra men, one for the left-field line and another for the right-field line. During the regular season we have a four-man crew. Everybody stays in the same order, so each of us has the same number of games at every position.

The late Bill Klem, who referred to himself as "the Old Arbitrator," was an exception. He worked the plate exclusively for sixteen consecutive seasons, a remarkable achievement. Klem estimated he had the plate every day for something like twenty-five hundred games, on the theory that he was better than his partners in calling balls and strikes. But I've also heard it said that he didn't work the bases because he had bad feet and couldn't move around too well.

Klem was a stern taskmaster and handled himself with great dignity. But he did have a sense of humor, which is also a necessity. On one occasion he ejected Pie Traynor, the great third baseman for the Pittsburgh Pirates. Traynor never used bad language, on or off the field. This rare ejection came as quite a surprise, and after the game the sportswriters hurried to the umpires' dressing room to find out what it was Traynor had said that prompted Klem to give Traynor the thumb.

"He wasn't feeling well," Klem reported.

"He looked okay before the game," one of the newspapermen said.

"Well"—Klem shrugged—"that's what he told me. He said he was sick of my stupid decisions."

Nowadays the league office considers all umpires equal in ability, so no umpire dominates the most difficult position. This is how it should be.

We rotate clockwise, the opposite of the way a player runs the bases. After a man works the plate, the next game he's at third base, not first base. Some people are confused by this, but there's a very good reason for it. If we did it the other way one man would have the two toughest assignments on doubleheaders. He'd have the plate in the opener and first base in the second game. He would be burdened with 90 percent of the decisions.

Next to the plate, first base is the busiest assignment. You get more bang-bang plays at first base than the other base positions. In a sense you're less involved than at the plate, but the pressure is the same. Balls and strikes are decided by a half-inch or an inch, sometimes by a quarter of an inch, and the only ones who can see the pitch as well as the umpire are the batter and the catcher. Many umpires believe they are judged and graded more on their base work, because the plays are more visible to the fans and the players.

There are no ties at first base. The runner beats it out or he doesn't. Some rule books say the tie goes to the runner, but I've never seen a rule that says when it's a tie you can holler, "Whoops, it's a tie! He's safe!" In our rule book there's no mention of a tie. You can go for months, maybe even a full season, and not have a tie.

First base is the only position where you take your eye off the ball, and you only do that at the end of the play. The first thing is to see where the throw is coming from, to pick up the ball, to be sure the throw is going to the first baseman. You set up at a ninety-degree angle to the throw. You don't want to be too close to the bag, but not too far away either. Fifteen to eighteen feet from the bag is best.

If the throw is off-target you readjust. If you see it's going to pull the first baseman off the bag—say, to the plate side—then you move closer to the plate, where you have better position to see if there is a tag. If the second baseman is making the throw and coming toward first, you move into foul territory. Otherwise you can get hit by the second baseman's throw. The same thing when the pitcher is covering. You move to the outside.

Once you know the throw is true, you take your eye off the ball and watch the bag. The first baseman is always set up first, so you see his feet first. Then you watch for the runner's foot and listen for the pop of the ball as it hits the first baseman's glove. You call the play by sound. Ninety times out of a hundred, there's a pop, even if the ball is in the dirt. It's the only way to do it. You can't watch the ball and the feet at the same time.

There is a big argument now going on about how the umpires should position themselves when working second base. There is a variance between the National and American leagues and I assume this traces back to the days of the two chiefs, Bill Klem, who was number one in the National League, and Tom Connolly, who was number one in the American. They were rivals, and whatever one league did, the other didn't.

In the National League we put our men in the infield. We call this working "inside," that is, you're on the edge of the grass, almost directly in front of the bag. If nobody is on base, we stay back, on the outfield side. We work inside only when there is a man on first base, or second base, or the bases are loaded. With a man on third base, we stay back.

In the American League they put their man behind the bag, regardless of the situation. They're fifteen to eighteen feet behind second base, on the edge of the outfield grass. You can argue from day to night which is best, but in my mind there's no question. It's better to work on the inside, and most other baseball men think so, too, because they teach the National League way in the umpire schools and use it in all the minor leagues. Even so, working on the outside does have advantages. In the American League they get a better shot on "trapped" balls, that is, when the outfielder catches the ball on a short, quick hop and then holds the ball in the air, as if he caught it on the fly. When you're behind second base, you're already in the outfield, so you've got better position on those types of plays.

The trapped ball can be tough. It helps if you listen for

the sound. If the man makes a clean catch sometimes you can hear the smack of the ball as it goes into the glove. But in this situation you can't rely totally on sound. The best way to make the call is from the side. This gives you a better angle. You don't want to be in a direct line with the ball.

The big argument against working inside is that we're more likely to get hit by line drives. I've been hit by line drives down the line, when I've been working first or third, but I've never been hit by a ball in the infield, not in twenty-five years in the National League. I've seen only two umpires hit by a line drive in that situation, Dusty Boggess and Babe Pinelli.

The plusses outweigh the minuses. When you're on the inside you get a better angle on the ball, especially on a steal, when the ball is thrown by the catcher, and on force plays. All we have to do is turn our head and the ball is in front of us. If you're in back of the play, the way they are in the American League, the umpires can't always see the ball. The fielder can juggle or drop the ball or the runner can kick it out of his glove, but the umpires might not see it until the ball rolls away and comes into their view.

The ball comes in from many different angles at second base. You've got force plays where the ball can be thrown from the pitcher, or the first or third baseman, and when you're in front of the play you've always got a good shot. Also you see the second baseman or the shortstop, whoever is covering, coming across the bag and the precise instant he catches the ball and touches the base.

Some American League umpires call these plays from the outside, but many of them run around the base and get into an inside position. To do this, they've got to circle the play and make a 180-degree turn.

Eventually, the American League will come around and do it our way. They'll change, just as they switched their position in 1974 against the inside chest protector and now allow their umpires the choice of using whichever protector is most comfortable for them. But on something like positioning, it can't be a matter of individual preference; it must be league policy. The younger umpires in the American League have had difficulty adjusting to working outside. It's contrary to all their previous training, and they've been pushing for a change.

Even when you're working inside, you can still boot a play. The last time this happened to me was when Joe Torre was on his last legs as a player with the New York Mets, a year or two before he was named the Met manager. Torre never did have good legs, not even when he was a kid. He was always one of the slowest runners in the National League.

In this particular game he tried to steal second. That alone surprised me. He came waddling in and went into a slide—bumpty de-bump, bumpty de-bump. Worst slide I ever saw. There was a big cloud of dust, and I made the cardinal sin in umpiring. I anticipated the play.

"You're out!"

Joe got up, hollering and screaming. "Tommy, I'm not out! I'm not out!"

"Joe, you're out," I said. "Get away from me."

"I'm not out!"

"Why not?"

"I've got the ball," he said, and he held up his hand. He had the ball all right. I could have dropped dead.

"What're you going to do now?" he asked.

I did all I could do. "You're out for interference," I said. "Get out of here."

"But, Tom, I didn't interfere with him. It was a clean slide."

All the time he's standing there holding the ball in the air for everyone to see.

I had to get out of it some way. An umpire can't admit to a player that he was wrong. So I changed my reasoning.

"You're out, Joe, because you've tagged yourself with the ball."

He walked away mumbling to himself.

Third base is the easiest position—if nothing is happening. But you can't go to sleep, because you never know what will happen next. Many times, in a close game, a call at third base is vital. The variety is there, too. All kinds of plays: throws from the outfield, bunts, force plays, tag plays, and appeal plays, usually when a runner leaves too early and tries to score on a fly to the outfield.

You also get traffic jams at third base, where two guys wind up standing on the bag. It happened to me in a Yankee-Dodger World Series game. It involved the Davis boys, Tommy and Willie.

Tommy was on first and Willie was the batter. Willie hit one down the right-field line. They took off. Willie could fly, maybe the fastest man on the bases in my time. But Willie had this bad habit of running with his head down. He didn't look up. So he came into third and, of course, Tommy was standing there. Two donkeys hung up at third base.

Tony Kubek, the television announcer, was playing shortstop for the Yankees at the time. Kubek got the ball from the outfield and walked over to tag them. I moved closer to see who he was going to tag. First Kubek tags Willie. Then he tags Tommy. Then he tags me. Why he tagged me, I'll never know.

And Kubek says, "One of you guys is out."

He was right. One guy was out. It was Willie Davis. The front man is always entitled to the bag.

Many fans don't seem to understand the appeal play. It doesn't come up very often, and only happens when a runner tags up on a fly ball. The runner can't leave the base until the catch is made. Only then can he try to advance to the next base. If he leaves early, the opposing team can appeal.

On this kind of play, the third-base umpire gets into foul territory and lines himself up so he can see both the runner and the man catching the ball. The slower runners are the ones likely to leave early.

Stan Musial left early once, on a fly ball to Richie Ashburn, when Ashburn was with the Phillies. Ashburn didn't have a strong arm. Musial took off before the ball hit Ashburn's glove. Puddinhead Jones was playing third base for the Phillies but he didn't appeal, and if there is no appeal, the umpire says nothing. The run scores. Smoky Burgess, a little fat man who could hit but couldn't run, was very good at leaving a split second too early. The opposing teams had a good "book" on Smoky. They always appealed.

The most spectacular plays—also the most important— are the tag plays at the plate. They can be tough. The advent of Astroturf has made it easier for the hitters, because ground balls skip through the infield much faster than on natural grass, and has brought about another change that I've never seen mentioned in the press. It's made for closer plays at the plate.

On natural grass, if there is a runner on second base with average or better than average speed, he should be able to score on a single to center or right field. To get him at the plate, the outfielder not only must make a hard and accurate throw, but he must get a true bounce so the catcher can handle the ball without difficulty. The ball is coming in at eighty miles an hour. Getting the true bounce is essentially a matter of luck.

On Astroturf and other artificial surfaces the catcher knows the bounce will be true and the ball will not veer to either side. Also, he's going to get the ball faster. And why not? There is no tall grass to slow up the ball when it's hit to the outfield, or when it's being thrown back to the infield.

When the umpire sees the play developing, the first thing he does is take off his mask. It would seem to be a simple thing, taking the mask off. But it takes two or three years for the new umpire to learn to do this. There's a trick to it, because you've got to take off your mask in such a way that it doesn't disturb your cap. You can't have your cap tumbling off. It can be a distraction and block your vision.

You don't jerk the mask off with one upward motion. First you pull it straight out from your forehead, then upward. The mask is taken off with the left hand, leaving the right hand free to make the call. If you held the mask in your right hand you could hit somebody in the head with it while you're making the call. You never see an umpire's mask on the ground. The only left-handed umpire who made the calls with his left hand was Jocko Conlan, and that was because he couldn't do it any other way. But if Jocko was starting today, he'd have to change.

The plate umpire also has an indicator that he uses to keep the count. The indicator is small enough to fit in the palm of the hand and helps you keep track of the number of outs and the count, the balls and strikes on each batter. I always held the indicator in my right hand, but most umpires hold it in their left hand.

Until last year I had heard of only one umpire who didn't use an indicator. He was Joe Cibulka from Chicago, who worked in the minor leagues for more than twenty years, most of it in the Western League. Cibulka was the Demosthenes of umpires. He kept five pebbles in his pockets, three large stones for balls and two smaller stones for strikes. And with every pitch he'd take the appropriate pebble out of his pocket and hold it in his hand. When his pockets were empty he had a full count.

Steve Palermo, one of the young American League umpires, also works without an indicator. He must be a math genius, or have an unusually retentive memory. His reasoning is as follows: the ball clubs now spend as much as one and two million dollars to build those big electronic scoreboards, so why shouldn't he take advantage of the new modern technology? When Palermo loses the count he picks it up from the scoreboard. An umpire shouldn't rely on the scoreboard operators. They don't always have the correct count. If a game is played from start to finish without delay we wouldn't need indicators either. But when there is an interruption it's easy either to forget or not to be absolutely certain of the count. Losing the count is not only embarrassing but unforgivable.

Another embarrassment is when you drop an extra ball or two on the field. We have special coats for working the plate, with wide and deep pockets to store the extra baseballs. You can hold three balls in each pocket. In hot weather, if we aren't wearing a coat, we have a small belt, with pockets on each side, like a holster.

Once, in a Dodger game, Billy Loes crossed up Roy Campanella on a pitch. The ball got away from Campy and hit me under the arm and then disappeared. I'm looking for the ball, Campy's looking for it. Nowhere in sight. Chuck Dressen, the Dodger manager, came out and joined in the search. Everybody was laughing like hell, having a good time. Three blind mice looking for the ball.

Finally, I said, "Wait a minute. Maybe it's in my pocket."

I knew I had five balls left and, sure enough, when I counted I had six.

There used to be a rule that whenever a pitcher would ask for a new ball we had to give it to him. Some pitchers always wanted a particular ball. Sal Maglie used to look for the high-seam ball. It gives you a better curveball. The baseballs are handsewn, and some of the seamstresses must be stronger than others. If they pull the stitches tighter, the seams are higher.

Maglie would drive me crazy. I gave him a new ball once, twice, then three times. He still wasn't satisfied. So I took six balls, three in each hand, and went to the mound and said, "Here, Sal, be my guest. Take your pick!"

We also have extra-wide pants for working the plate, so we can be comfortable in a squat. You tell the tailor what you want and he makes the seat bigger. Harry Wendelstedt, a fine National League umpire, didn't know about this, and made the mistake of ordering his uniform from a sporting-goods catalogue.

Harry was fresh out of the Al Somers Umpiring School and had his first plate game. He was all excited. It was the opening game of the season in Brunswick, Georgia, in the Georgia-Florida League. The pants were so tight they fit like leotards. Harry bent down, getting into position for the very first pitch, and he heard this loud rip. The seam of the pants split in half. The crowd howled. The next day in the Brunswick paper there was a picture on the front page, taken from behind the screen, that showed Harry's rear end with a big white patch showing through his torn pants. The headline above the picture said:

"OFFICIAL OPENING."

eople say to me, "Tom, are you ever wrong?"

"No, I'm never wrong. I can't be wrong on my job. But I've made mistakes. I'm a human being. I could be wrong, but when I call a play that's the way I see it."

Many years ago, in Vero Beach, Florida, where the Dodgers train, the General Electric Company came down and set up a magic eye. They put it behind the plate, to call the pitches. Pee Wee Reese, the Dodgers' star shortstop, and one of the best I've seen, stood at the plate and, in a sense, went against the magic eye. It flashed when the pitches were in the strike zone. Pee Wee was a very good hitter, a very keen eye. But he struck out three times in a row—according to the machine. Pee Wee didn't believe the machine. He never cussed, but I remember him saying, "Take that damn machine out of here."

I don't think they'll ever use cameras instead of officials in baseball. God forbid. If they ever take the human element out of baseball, they'll be taking the heart out of the game. If you watched a game where the cameras called the plays, you wouldn't enjoy it.

First, you'd have nobody to boo or holler at; second, the camera isn't always right. It depends on the camera angle. Let's say the bases are loaded, one out or no outs, and the runners are running. The ball's alive. What are you going to do? Hold up all the runners and say, "Now wait a minute. Freeze right there. We've got to move the camera."

The instant replay has become a big part of the enjoyment of watching sports on television. But the overall effect has been beneficial to umpires. More than anything else, it shows that we're right 98, 99 percent of the time. And don't forget, when they show an instant replay they're usually repeating a very close play, a bang-banger.

I remember one World Series game in Pittsburgh, the year Roberto Clemente had that great Series. There were five or six tough calls in one game, and the umpires got every one of them right.

One play in particular stands out in my memory. It was a line drive into the right-field corner—a shot. Johnny Rice, an American League umpire from Chicago, had the right-field line. We used to call Rice "Mayor Daley." His resemblance to the late Chicago mayor was remarkable. He could have been his twin brother.

Rice called it a foul ball. There was a big rhubarb. They repeated that play on television all night. But you couldn't tell by the cameras. Half the TV announcers said Rice was wrong, the other half insisted he was right. That's how close it was.

Bob Miller, a Pittsburgh relief pitcher, was sitting in

the Pirate bullpen and had the best shot at the ball. He was closer than anybody else. The ball went right over Miller's head. The next day Miller admitted Johnny Rice made the correct call.

In other team sports—football, basketball, tennis, soccer—the chalk lines are out of bounds. In baseball, the lines are in bounds. Tony Cuccinello, a very good third-base coach, once said baseball should change the language in the rule books. He said the foul lines should be called the "fair lines," and he's right. If the ball hits the line, it's a fair ball.

In football, a player goes up into the air and catches a pass and maybe he's two feet inbounds when he catches the ball. But when he comes down, if his feet are on the line or the other side of the line, he's out-of-bounds and it doesn't count. He's offside. It's a bad rule. They should go by the position of the ball. Where the ball is caught is important. That's the way we call it in baseball.

We now have forty-foot flagpoles down the foul lines. These "fair poles," as Cuccinello would call them, have an attached three-foot screen. The screens are in fair territory. We fought for these screens for many years. You've got a guy hitting a ball 350 or 400 feet, or more, and the ball is curving. It's a tough call. It breeds a lot of argument.

If the ball hits the screen, or the pole, it's a home run. It makes it easy for us. There is no question, no argument. Many times the ball soars above the pole. We make the call according to where the ball was when it cleared the pole. A ball can curve foul and land ten or fifteen feet on the foul side, but it's a home run. And there's no time to stop and develop a picture. It's either fair or foul.

No umpire can possibly get every play right. We're not perfect, though I've heard it said an umpire is supposed to be perfect his first day on the job and then show constant improvement. And if we miss a play there's no way we can make it up. Only a bad umpire tries to make up a bad play, that is, call the next play for the other team to even it up.

And you can't admit to a player or to a manager you blew a play. If you do this you lose your credibility. An umpire should never ask for mercy, or ask to be forgiven. A ball field isn't a church. Players aren't parishioners coming to confess their sins. They're hard-nosed professionals, and the one big difference between the professional and amateur is that the professional has to win, or come damn close.

There is always pressure. From the moment you step on the field, the tension builds, especially in the big games— All-Star games, playoff games, the World Series. But you'd be surprised how the tension leaves you once you get into the game. Suddenly your mind is on the game. You're so absorbed in what you're doing, everything else is blocked out and you calm down.

And once the game is over, you must forget about it. A good game or a bad game, you can't carry it with you. If you do, one of two things will happen. Either you'll get overconfident, or, if you've had a bad day, you'll start to lose your confidence. Never go home with a game. It'll cause trouble with your wife and family. If you've got to talk about it, if you've had a tough play, talk it over with your partners.

There's still another rule. If a young umpire has a tough play and asks me about it, I don't play the good guy and tell him, "Oh, sure, you made a good call. Perfect call." If he kicked it, I tell him. It'll help him become a better umpire. We all see the play from a different perspective. I never con a young umpire, but I never say anything, either, unless he asks me.

Our only job, the principal reason we're on the field, is to see the game is played according to the rules and to get the plays right. This means there are times when an umpire must reverse his decision. And when an umpire reverses himself he should never consider it an embarrassment. Look at it this way: the ballplayers miss a lot more plays than we do. According to a recent study the umpires are right on 98 percent of the plays.

We can't see everything. We have a rule in the books, for instance, which states that anytime we're blocked out of a play at home plate we should look to our partners and they'll give us the sign.

Say I've got a tough play at the plate. The runner is coming in standing up, the catcher makes the tag. Big collision. They spin each other around. Or they roll over on the ground.

I see the tag and I call the runner out. But I'm blocked out. What I don't see is that the catcher, after making the tag, dropped the ball.

Immediately we hear it from the dugout.

"He dropped the ball! He dropped the ball."

They're so emphatic that you say to yourself, "Wait a minute, maybe they're right. I'll ask my partner."

So I'll look to my partner. Say it's Billy Williams, a fine umpire. We worked together on the same crew for eleven years. If he gives me the sign that the runner is safe, I'll turn around and announce, "I'm reversing my decision." But I announce the reversing. Not my partner.

The same thing with a ball going into the outfield and you've got two umpires making a double call, one safe, one out. One umpire says the outfielder trapped the ball, the other calls it a catch. The first thing we do is get the players away. We never talk to the players; we don't want their opinions. We go to another umpire, the next man nearest to the play, or to the man who had the best view. It's his baby. He makes the final decision.

There are also times when all four umpires will gather behind second base, after a rhubarb, and when this happens we are discussing a rule situation. Surprising as it may seem, there are some rules that, to some small degree, contradict each other. There can be two interpretations. On some of the rules you've got to be a Philadelphia lawyer. This is a sore point with the umpires because, so far as I know, an umpire has never been a member of the Official Rules Committee. It doesn't make sense, really, because it's our job to interpret the rules. But this is being corrected, to some extent. The members of the Rules Committee lately have agreed to consult with us. Anyway, when we're meeting at second base, or wherever, the four of us are determining the most logical interpretation. If possible, we don't want the game to continue under protest.

The last few years we've had the "half-swing," and that's become the toughest call. It's the umpire's judgment whether or not the batter swung at the ball. The ballplayers and the managers, many of them, tell you it's not a swing unless the batter breaks his wrists.

I've had players say, "I didn't break my wrists, how can you call it a swing?"

But I've seen fellows get base hits without breaking their wrists. If the bat comes more than halfway around the plate, it's a swing, so long as the bat crosses the plate. A checked swing is when the batter brings the bat back before it crosses the plate. But there are times when a batter is ducking away from a pitch, and in so doing his bat may cross the plate. We don't consider that a swing. It's an accident.

When the half-swing rule first came in, it was a good rule. It was limited to "any questionable swing," and only the manager could appeal. Most managers were fair, but others, like Sparky Anderson, took advantage. Sparky asked on everything.

If we called it a ball and the manager disagreed, he could say, "Tom, I want to ask your first-base partner or your third-base partner if he swung." On right-handed hitters we ask the first-base umpire; on left-handed, the third-base umpire. But only the manager could ask.

The next year they allowed the catcher to ask. Now everybody asks. They made a joke out of it. The pitcher's hollering, the catcher's hollering, the infield's hollering, the whole bench is hollering. All we hear is, "Ask your partner. Ask your partner." And we have to ask. Even if I'm positive that the batter didn't swing, we must honor every appeal. The decision of the base umpire is binding.

Beanball and knockdown pitchers are another problem. It used to be routine for a pitcher to knock a player down if the player was hitting exceptionally well. It's part of the game. If a player hits a home run, or gets a few big hits in a row, he expects to go down his next time at bat. There's all kinds of names for these pitches: beanball, knockdown, and so on.

It's very seldom, extremely seldom, that a pitcher throws a beanball and actually aims for the batter's head. That's dangerous stuff, and everybody knows it. In all the long history of major-league baseball, only one player was killed by a beanball, a fellow named Ray Chapman. That was many, many years ago. To prevent a reoccurrence, the players now wear protective helmets. Going to helmets was a good idea. It made it a safer game.

Some pitchers knock the hitters down or brush them back just to let them know they're out there. Dizzy Dean was very good at this. He'd always knock the first batter down. Didn't matter who the hitter was. Down he'd go. Big Bill Lee of Chicago was another one. If a guy got two hits in a row off Bob Gibson, the third time he'd go down. It was automatic. Don Newcombe of the Dodgers pitched that way, too.

In these situations, the umpires are on the spot. If, in our opinion, we think a pitcher is deliberately throwing at a batter, we immediately warn him, a warning that also carries an automatic fifty-dollar fine. But the problem is this: the pitchers always insist they aren't throwing at anybody. When they hit someone their explanation is always the same: "The ball got away." In other words, they lost their control. Many times this is true. The point, though, is that we can't be certain in this situation. We can never be sure what the pitcher is thinking. We're not mind readers.

Some years ago, when Don Drysdale was in his prime, he knocked down Frank Robinson. Frank was having a big day. Drysdale threw his best fastball—and he had a great fastball. It hit Robinson's helmet. Down he went. He was out cold.

I told Drysdale that I believed he had thrown at Robinson deliberately. Drysdale swore it was unintentional. "The ball just got away." Both benches emptied and there was a big free-for-all. When the fighting stopped, I went to the Dodgers' bench and told Walter Alston, their manager, that Drysdale was being fined fifty dollars and if he did it again I'd not only throw him out of the game, but Walter would go with him.

Drysdale threatened to sue me and the National League president because of my accusation. No umpire wants to be involved in that kind of situation. For that reason, we're very cautious. Still, the veteran umpire—not always, but usually—can tell when a pitcher is deliberately throwing at a hitter. Most of the time, though, the pitcher just brushes the batter back off the plate, and that's legitimate.

If I was a pitcher I'd never knock down a good hitter. You're not going to scare a good hitter by throwing at him. All you're doing is getting him twice as mad at you. One year, in 1957, Ernie Banks of the Chicago Cubs was knocked down four times by four different pitchers. Don Drysdale, Bob Purkey, Bob Friend, and Jack Sanford—all of them took a shot at him. And each time he was knocked down Banks hit their next pitch out of the park. That's the truth. You can look it up.

When Sal Maglie was pitching for Brooklyn he took a couple of shots at Willie Mays. I had the plate that day. Maglie's first pitch wasn't all that close, but it was a genuine brushback. Willie went down on the next pitch, a duster.

I went to the mound and told Maglie, "There'll be no more of that. The next one you throw, you're going to go with the ball."

Sal says, "Tom, it's a hot night, I'm sweating like hell. The ball just got away from me."

I said, "Bullshit," and started back to home plate.

Maglie says, "Hey, Tom?"

"Yeah, what do you want?"

"Tell Willie I'm sorry."

I get back to the plate. Willie is still brushing himself off. I said, "Willie, Maglie says he's sorry."

Willie had that high-pitched voice. He gave me sort of a quizzical look and said, "Is that right?"

This was in Brooklyn, at Ebbets Field, and Willie hit the next pitch out on Bedford Avenue, a four-hundred-foot home run.

And when Willie was rounding second base he yelled, "Hey, Maglie, I'm sorry."

When there is a fight on the field, 90 percent of the time it's because of a beanball or knockdown pitch. The pitchers aren't always to blame. They're goaded into retaliation by their manager and teammates. If an opposing pitcher knocks down one of his teammates, a player expects his pitcher to get even and knock down the other pitcher, or one of the opposition players. It's part of the baseball code.

Many times a pitcher is reluctant to respond, because when he comes to bat he's running the risk of getting hit.

This is no longer a problem in the American League, because they've got the designated hitter rule and the pitchers don't come to bat. Still, the number of knockdown and beanball pitches is diminishing. It's become a matter of economics. The players are making good money, many of them big money, and they don't want to get hurt and jeopardize their careers. Even if a guy isn't directly involved in a knockdown rhubarb he can be injured in the free-for-all that is almost certain to follow.

Another constant controversy is the spitball and other illegal pitches such as the Vaseline ball, also known as the greaseball. The rule book is very explicit: A pitcher cannot bring his hand in contact with his mouth or lips while he's in the eighteen-foot circle surrounding the pitcher rubber; also he cannot apply a foreign substance of any kind to the ball; he cannot expectorate on the ball, or his hand, or his glove; or rub the ball on his glove, person, or clothing; or deface the ball in any manner.

What a joke! Almost every team has at least one pitcher who throws the spitter or the greaseball. Some teams may have as many as two or three greaseball pitchers. They all cheat. And you can't blame the umpires. The people at fault are the league presidents. When an umpire once tried to clean it up, he was left hanging. The league office didn't support him.

In the middle 1960s, Chris Pelekoudas, a very good umpire, decided he would stop the cheaters. Chris knew that two pitchers in particular, Gaylord Perry, who was then with the San Francisco Giants, and Phil Regan of the Chicago Cubs, were constantly throwing the greaser or spitter. When the opposing managers complained, and they were always complaining, the plate umpire had to stop the game and go to the mound and search the pitcher to see if he could find a foreign substance either on his glove or on his person. We became detectives.

The pitcher had to remove his cap, sometimes his shirt. This "undressing" of the pitcher was a common scene. But it was embarrassing to us because we could never find evidence of a foreign substance. The fans laughed. So did the players. Five, ten minutes later, the game would resume, and the very next pitch would be another greaseball. The whole thing made us look like a bunch of clowns.

The pitchers used a variety of foreign substances, not just spit. They used white toothpaste, Vaseline, even vaginal jelly. Once we found a tube of Vaseline in Gaylord Perry's warm-up jacket, but this was considered circumstantial evidence, not enough to convict. The pitchers would put the stuff on their foreheads, on their arms, on their belts, on their necks. You don't need a big lump of the stuff. Just a little dab. A little dab would do it.

Pelekoudas, a very proud man, decided he had enough of the Barnum and Bailey routine. One night, on a flight to Chicago, he discussed the situation with his partners. They reached an agreement; they would base their judgment on "the flight of the ball." In other words, if they thought the pitch looked like a spitter or greaseball, the pitcher would be penalized accordingly. No more searches.

The next day Pelekoudas had the plate. It was a close game. Durocher was managing the Cubs and called Regan in from the bullpen. Regan, of course, needed the spitter. It was his out pitch. Pelekoudas penalized Regan on three or four successive pitches. Pete Rose struck out on one of these pitches, but Pelekoudas ruled it an illegal pitch and Rose was allowed another swing.

The Cubs protested and called Warren Giles, the league president. I'll never forget it. Mr. Giles was in Rochester, New York, making a speech. He caught the next flight to Chicago and the next morning met with Pelekoudas and his partners. Pelekoudas was advised he couldn't make any such judgments because, in effect, he was accusing

Regan, "a fine Christian gentleman," of cheating without any clear evidence. And—get this—Pelekoudas had to apologize to Regan!

Regan has since retired, with honors, and so has Pelekoudas. But Gaylord Perry is still going strong, at the age of forty, and may be the first pitcher since Early Wynn to win three hundred big-league games.

A few years back, when Gaylord was traded from the Giants to the Cleveland Indians, some of his friends threw a party for him in Redwood City, California. Guess who they asked to be the principal speaker? My old friend Chris Pelekoudas. Chris made a very nice speech and, at the finish, handed Gaylord a going-away present, something to take with him into the American League. It was a five-pound jar of Vaseline.

But before Chris retired he did have one big satisfaction. Mr. Chub Feeney, who succeeded Warren Giles as president of the National League, agreed that the rule should be changed. Now an umpire can penalize a pitcher by watching "the flight of the ball."

The hassle over illegal pitches is eternal, endless. Last summer Doug Harvey, a veteran and knowledgeable umpire, tried to clean up Don Sutton's act. Sutton is a very good pitcher, been with the Dodgers for years, a big winner. But he has this habit of defacing and cutting the ball. Been doing it for years. Harvey never caught him in the act, but in one game he penalized him ten or fifteen times.

Sutton yelled for his lawyer, and Tommy LaSorda, the Dodger manager, yelled for the league president, insisting his pitcher was being unjustly accused. And Mr. Feeney had to admit there was no proof it was actually Sutton who was defacing the balls. He said it could have been one of his teammates. I don't know. Maybe Mr. Feeney thought it was an act of God. Mr. Feeney didn't support Harvey. Now they tell me that Sutton has gone back to the spitter and that he only cuts three or four balls every time he pitches.

9

Working the plate is the toughest assignment for an umpire. We make about 250 to 300 calls a game on balls and strikes. Sometimes the tension mounts and you get into a heavy situation. Whenever possible, I'd always try to inject a little humor. It can loosen things up.

Emmett Ashford was the major leagues' first black umpire. He was in the American League, and the only unfortunate aspect about it was that by the time he got to the big leagues he was already in his fifties, close to retirement age. It's too bad he didn't have a longer major-league career.

The only time I worked with Emmett, when we were

partners, was in spring training. One day we had the Baltimore Orioles in Miami, Florida. I had the plate and Emmett was working first base. Brooks Robinson, the Baltimore superstar, was at bat and swung at the pitch. A feeble swing—but a swing.

Brooks stepped back and said, "Tom, I don't think I swung."

"Brooks, baby, you swung at the ball. I saw it."

Brooks said, "Tom, will you do me a favor? Will you ask Emmett?"

The rule is clear. On a situation where there is the possibility of a half-swing, the batter is entitled to appeal. I relayed his appeal to Ashford.

"Yeah, man," Emmett shouted, "he swung at the ball."

I turned to Brooks and said, "Okay, Brooks, now you've got it in black and white."

The most frequent calls—balls and strikes—are obviously the potential troublemakers. It's the pitch on or off the corners, or an inch too high or too low, that triggers most of the rhubarbs. The book says the strike zone is from the armpit to the top of the knees, but in actuality you can't go by the book. You have to go by the position that the batter hits from, his stance. Not everyone's strike zone is the same.

When a hitter stands straight up, he's going to have a bigger strike zone. Joe DiMaggio hit straight up. So did Willie Mays. Ted Williams, another of the great hitters, had a big strike zone. The guy with the biggest strike zone, in my time, was Frank Howard. Howard is six feet eight inches—he had been a star basketball player at Ohio State—and he barely bent over. But even with that big strike zone, the pitchers were afraid to pitch to him. Everybody was afraid of Frank. But like most big fellows, he has a gentle temperament. I heard that one time, when he was with the Dodgers, he grabbed Durocher by the neck and threatened to pinch his head off.

Some hitters, to give themselves the edge, bend over in a crouch. Musial hit out of a crouch. Pete Rose, the long-time Cincinnati star now with the Phillies, always bends over, to give the pitchers a smaller target. But Rose is pretty cute. Once the pitch is on its way he begins straightening up. When he does that, the size of the strike zone increases accordingly.

I didn't see too much of Gene Woodling. He was in the American League, and he was one of the big crouchers. The guy with the smallest strike zone was Bill Veeck's midget, Eddie Gaedel. He was about three and a half feet tall. When Veeck sent him up to pinch-hit, the first thing he did was get into a crouch. A funny little guy.

We didn't have any midgets in the National League, but we always had a lot of small guys. Eddie Stanky was a little fellow, and he had a great eye. Stanky would lead the league, or be among the leaders, in walks every year. We had to cure Stanky of one of his cute habits. When the count would go to three balls, he'd anticipate ball four and would start running to first base before the pitch got to the plate. He'd try to talk you into the pitch. Whenever he did that, if the pitch was close, anywhere close, we'd call it a strike. We'd tell him, "C'mon back, Charlie." Stanky was a bright guy. After a while he got the message.

You would think the smaller guys would be a bigger problem for the pitchers because of their tiny strike zone. But the small guys seldom are home-run threats, so the pitchers can just fog 'em in, let 'em hit it. One recent exception is Joe Morgan, the Cincinnati second baseman. He's one of the few little guys who can hit the ball a long way. I don't know where Morgan gets his power from, but it's there.

Most of the better hitters wait on the pitch. It's the .220 hitters who commit themselves early and lunge at the ball. The good hitter doesn't start his swing until the last possible split second. By waiting, he gets a better and longer look at the ball. Ted Williams always said he saw the ball when it hit his bat, at the instant of impact. A lot of people in baseball never believed him, but I did. Because of these late swingers, it's important that an umpire never anticipate the pitch. You wait, too. If you're too quick with your call it can be embarrassing.

When Henry Aaron was going for Babe Ruth's record, the league office sent us what we called "Henry Aaron balls." They were marked with invisible ink and kept in a special bag. The league did this to be sure that the ball being returned was authentic. Nobody wanted a phony ball in the Hall of Fame. There were times when Henry would hit one into the seats and ten kids would show up, all claiming they had the ball. We began using the special balls when Henry passed the seven hundred mark.

The game would be delayed when Henry came to bat. One night in September 1973, Dutch Rennert, who had the plate, dropped a few of the Henry Aaron balls. Rennert apologized and told Henry, "Switching these balls makes me nervous."

Hank laughed. "If you think you're nervous," he said, "how do you think I feel?"

Henry tied the record the following year, in his first game of the 1974 season. Eddie Vargo had the plate. When Henry hit number 715, which broke the record, Ed Sudol had the plate. Didn't surprise any of us. Sudol always seemed to be involved in historic games.

Sudol also had the plate when Jim Bunning pitched a perfect game against the New York Mets. A perfect game, of course, is a much greater rarity than a no-hitter. In a perfect game nobody reaches base—twenty-seven batters, twenty-seven consecutive outs. Bunning was one of the star pitchers of his time, but he wasn't a friend of the umpires. He used to squeeze a lot. Everything had to be a strike.

Harvey Haddix, a super guy, also pitched one of the few

perfect games in National League history. Haddix was a gentleman. He always said hello, how are you. He regarded umpires as human beings. Haddix worked at his position. There are very few pitchers who are outstanding fielders, but Haddix was one of them. So was Bobby Shantz. Freddie Fitzsimmons was also a great fielder, for a pitcher.

I had the plate in five no-hitters. I had Carl Erskine, Warren Spahn, Lew Burdette, and Bill Stoneman. I can't remember the fifth guy. A pitcher has to be lucky to get a no-hitter. Everything has to go right. Usually when you're working a no-hitter, you don't even know it. I remember when Stoneman was pitching his no-hitter, John Bateman, his catcher, said to me, "Stoney's throwing the ball good."

I said, "Yeah, he's got good stuff."

Then Bateman said, "They haven't had a hit off him yet."

"Is that right?" I didn't even realize it and we were already in the seventh or eighth inning.

Over the years, I was probably on the field in ten or twelve no-hitters. I had the left-field line when Don Larsen of the Yankees pitched his perfect no-hitter against the Dodgers, the only no-hitter in World Series history. I had the plate the day before, so in a sense I missed his by one day.

I didn't realize the Dodgers hadn't had a hit off Larsen until the eighth inning. I was walking up and down the left-field line when the teams were changing sides. Frankie Crosetti, the Yankees' third-base coach, said, "Tom, do you think Larsen will make it?"

"Make what?"

And he said, "He's got a perfect game going."

Usually, but not always, the best pitchers give you the least trouble. Sandy Koufax was wonderful. When he first came up he was wild, really wild. There were times when he couldn't even hit the backstop. You've got to give him credit, because he worked hard on his game. Everything he got he deserved. He never complained, not even in his younger days when he didn't have control. I never saw him show a temper. He was a dream. When Koufax was pitching it was either a called strike or a swinging strike. He was smart. He always tried to throw as few pitches as possible. And he had the best curveball, for a left-hander, that I ever saw, what we used to call the old drop. It broke down and in on the right-handed batters. There were times when a hitter was lucky if he was able to get a foul off him.

I remember reading a story in the *Sporting News* during the winter that Gene Oliver, the catcher, hit .330 against Sandy Koufax. I couldn't believe it. Oliver was a .220 hitter. Besides, he was a left-handed hitter, and lefties seldom got a hit off Koufax.

I saw Oliver the next year, in spring training. I couldn't wait to see him. I said, "Gene, I want to ask you something. How in the world could you hit .330 against Koufax?"

Oliver laughed and said, "Tom, I'll tell you, but it's a secret. Don't tell anybody. He thinks I'm Jewish."

Juan Marichal, who had an outstanding career with the San Francisco Giants, was almost in Koufax's class. But he didn't have Koufax's temperament. Actually, Marichal was a pain—anything close he wanted. But he knew how to pitch. He hid the ball until the last split second, and he had that double-pump windup. He was a man of many deliveries and could throw the same pitch from three different places. He threw straight overhand, three-quarters, and sidearm, and he could throw each of his pitches at two or three different speeds. A master craftsman. He was a pretty good bench jockey, too. I unloaded him once from the dugout.

He said, "Me no saying nothing, Tom."

I said, "Good-bye. See you tomorrow."

Jim Maloney, who pitched a couple of no-hitters when he was with Cincinnati, was another good one, but he got to moaning when he was at the end of his career. Don Drysdale was tough, but good. Toward the end Drysdale loaded up a few. I'd say he had a very good spitter, just like Gaylord Perry's. But Drysdale didn't seem to use it as much as Perry, just when he needed a strikeout, or when he was in a jam in the late innings.

Ferguson Jenkins, who was a twenty-game winner six years in a row when he was with the Cubs, was also one of the best. For some reason Jenkins never got the national publicity he deserved. He was steady and he had great control. He could hit the corners. The Cubs traded him away. They tell me Jenkins is now throwing what the players call a "dirt ball," that is, he scrubs dirt into the seams and the ball drops straight down, like a spitter. That's a new one on me. I'd never heard of a dirt ball before.

I got along pretty good with Tom Seaver, the pinup boy. But we had our ups and downs. He's sixty feet six inches from the plate, and I'm only a foot and a half; it's incredible how much better his eyesight is than mine. He can holler. And he's got another cute habit. If he thinks you've missed a pitch, he stands out there and stares at you. Sometimes I think maybe he should have been a hypnotist.

If I had to have a pitcher for one game I'd probably go with Bob Gibson, who had all those great years with the St. Louis Cardinals. He'd fight you all the way. An absolutely marvelous competitor. And Gibson knew how to pace himself. He was one of the very few pitchers whose fastball was as good in the eighth and ninth innings as it was in the first and second.

I had the plate in the 1968 World Series game when Gibson went against Denny McLain of Detroit, a match-up of two great pitchers. This was the game that Gibson had seventeen strikeouts, a World Series record. I didn't realize Gibson had all those strikeouts and afterwards a reporter said to me, "Hey, Tom, what do you think of that? Gibson struck out seventeen batters."

I said, "No, he didn't get that many. Not seventeen."

"Yes, he did."

So I said, "He did like hell. He got ten and I got seven." Seven of those were on called strikes.

This guy put that in his paper, and a couple of days later Commissioner Bowie Kuhn calls me and wanted to know what I was saying, not realizing it was just a joke. That story must have gone all over the country, because when I was on the banquet circuit that winter people were saying to me, "I didn't know umpires helped out pitchers."

Believe me, Mr. Gibson didn't need any help.

A couple of years later, in the early seventies, I got to know Gibson better. He and I and Johnny Bench and Art Reichle, the baseball coach at UCLA, went to Europe together. We were there for a month, running baseball clinics for the armed forces. Gibson instructed the pitchers, Bench took the catchers, and Reichle had the infielders and outfielders. I was the moderator and also ran a clinic for the umpires.

It was cold over there. This was in January. Johnny Bench wore a big fur coat with a hood on it. It was one of Bench's prize possessions. The year before Bench had toured Alaska with Bob Hope and Bob gave him this coat. I think Bench slept in it, too.

For the first week or two Gibson was annoyed because the guards at the borders were always asking him for his passport. He thought they were picking on him because he's black. So he and Bench switched passports. They still stopped him, and Bench, too. And the funny thing about it is that the guards would look at their passports, never ask a question, and just give them back.

My last time around the league, in 1976, when I was retiring, I wanted a couple of autographed balls of the Cincinnati club. So I gave them to the ball boy and told him to take them to Johnny Bench and tell him to have the boys sign them for me. Two minutes later the kid comes back with the balls. The kid's got a long face.

"What's the matter? Didn't they sign the balls?"

He said, "Johnny Bench told me to tell you the only time the team signs balls is when they're on the road. They don't sign them at home anymore. It's a new rule."

I'd never heard of such a rule. An hour later we're into the game. Bench is hitting number five and he comes up in the second inning. I had a 2–2 pitch on him, half on the black, half on the white. I said to myself, "What the hell, it's close enough."

I called Bench out. He looked at me in disgust and walked away. He puts the tools back on and comes back to the plate and says, "Hey, Tom, I thought that ball was outside."

I said, "John, sign the balls."

"That ball came in at ninety-five miles an hour. It was going too fast to sign."

"I'm not talking about the pitch. I'm talking about the balls I sent to the clubhouse before the game."

"Oh," Bench said, "send 'em over tomorrow. They'll be signed."

It was a funny thing. He seldom argued with the umpires, but he got chased more than a few times. Every time manager Sparky Anderson got chased, Bench got chased, too. Sparky would come out with a big beef and Bench would join in.

It was easy to work the plate behind Bench, because he got down low. The guy who caught at Cincinnati before him, Johnny Edwards, was tough. Edwards couldn't bend down. He didn't catch in a squat. Walker Cooper of the Cardinals was the same way. He was such a big man, he couldn't get down. He tried, eventually, and would get down on one leg, but even then he'd block your vision.

Wes Westrum was another guy who was tough to work

behind. Westrum never used the whole plate. He would always sit on the outside corner. Durocher wanted him to catch that way. Durocher didn't want his pitchers throwing the ball inside, and so Westrum used only half the plate. It made for a lot of arguments.

Another thing we don't like is when a catcher holds a pitch. If they don't like the call, they can ask, "Where was it?" or something like that, but we don't want them showing us up, and that's what they're doing when they're holding the ball. Jerry Grote, who was with the Mets for many years, had a reputation for holding pitches. The fifth or sixth time he did it to me, he happened to bend down and I kicked him.

"Hey, what'd you kick me for?" he asked.

"Oh, excuse me," I said. But he didn't hold any more pitches.

To me, the best catcher I worked behind was Roy Campanella, the great star of the old Brooklyn Dodgers. Campy knew how to catch and he stayed down very well. He'd give you a good shot at the ball. The main thing about working the plate is to get a look at the pitch as it's coming in, to see it all the way.

If a catcher is bouncing and, say, a guy is stealing, the instinctive move for the catcher is to come up and catch the ball and throw it, especially if he sees the runner has a good jump. And when they come up they take you out of the pitch. A lot of fans don't realize this, but we've got to go up with the catcher and get that last look. And if the umpire is small and the catcher's a big guy, the umpire could have trouble.

Some umpires work closer to the catcher than others. Sometimes when you're too close, the catcher will say, "Tom, you're on my back. Give me some room."

But they don't realize that once we get a shot at the pitch we back up. Shag Crawford, who is now retired, worked closer than anybody. Shag would get down in his squat and put his hand on the catcher's back, to level himself and keep his balance. That was his style. All umpires have their own style.

The National League umpires have always had more mobility because we use the inside chest protector. For years, the American League umpires had to use the outside protector. Again, it goes back to Bill Klem and Tom Connolly. Klem wore the inside protector and Connolly the outside protector, and so all the umpires in each league had to follow the leader. It was a tradition. It was also ridiculous.

We call the outside protector a balloon. You blow it up. You raise it up and push it under your chin. It does give you more protection, especially of the arms and upper torso. But it's so bulky you can't bend, at least not too far. The most you can do is bow at the waist. You can't squat, so you have to work over the catcher's head. In our league we work over the shoulder, over the catcher's right shoulder when the hitter is right-handed, and over the left shoulder for left-handed hitters. The inside protector is much smaller. It's padded, like a waffle. You wear it inside your shirt. The fans can't see it.

The American League put an end to this nonsense in 1974 and advised its umpires they could wear the protector of their choice, whichever was more comfortable for them. Four years later, half the American League umpires were using the inside protector. In time they'll all be using it. And when they do, it'll put an end to the old wives' tale that the two leagues have different strike zones.

The ballplayers, the managers, the sportswriters believe this. But they're wrong. It just isn't true. The assumption is that in the National League the pitcher gets the low strike, that we have a lower strike zone because the umpire can get down. The American League umpires supposedly give the pitchers a higher strike. But they don't know what they're talking about.

Logically, it might seem that way because the National League umpires, as a group, do work lower, and so it's natural to assume they have a tendency to bring the ball down. But despite what appears to be logic, the fact is that we all have what is essentially the same strike zone. When working the plate, the umpire does not move his body. Only the eyes move, because if you move your body you could lose sight of the ball. There might be a variance of an inch or two, according to the style of the individual umpire, but this variance occurs in both leagues.

I've never heard anybody say there is a different strike zone in the minor leagues—and *all* umpires start in the minors. Umpires from both leagues work the All-Star game and the World Series, and very seldom do we get any arguments about the so-called high or low strike. Yet I can talk from now until kingdom come and they'll say, "You're wrong, Tom."

I've also heard it said that the National League umpires, because they work low, have trouble seeing the pitch on the outside corner. But we never work that low. You set yourself up so you can see the entire plate.

The toughest thing in sports is to hit a baseball thrown by a professional pitcher. They can make it curve and slide and they can make it back up. The ball is always moving and breaking and it is thrown at speeds of from eighty-five to ninety-five miles an hour. We have had guys sit behind the plate and time the pitches with radar guns. It's a very subtle game the way the professionals play it.

In order to hit the ball well, you've got to hit it squarely, which is very difficult. If you don't hit squarely, you pop up, or hit on the ground, or miss the ball completely. It's an accomplishment just to hit the ball.

The easiest games to work are with two veteran pitchers who throw strikes. It's the kids who don't have control who make the job tougher. But you never let a ballplayer know you think he's a poor or mediocre player. The level of their ability is not your concern. The umpire is there to call the plays, not to make judgments on anybody's ability. Anyway, today's kid pitcher is tomorrow's star.

For some reason left-handers are wilder than right-handers. I've never seen a left-hander who could throw a ball straight. That's why they call them "crooked arms." The ball dips and sails and jumps all over. I've always tried to be extra patient with young left-handers who have trouble throwing strikes. I guess it's because I had the same problem myself.

Some fans—and players and managers, too—are convinced that the superstars are always getting the breaks from the umpires. I remember Birdie Tebbetts saying this at a banquet one night. Birdie had been a player and manager of a couple of major-league clubs, a bright guy, and he said, "You know, you guys are always giving the superstars four strikes."

"You're all wrong, Birdie," I told him. "The superstars don't need four strikes. All they need is one."

It's the humpty-dumpty hitters, the guys with the .210 average, who do 90 percent of the beefing. They always say the same thing. They turn around and say, "How can that be a strike?"

I give them all the same answer. "Look at the scoreboard and see for yourself."

It may seem surprising, but Leo Durocher wasn't the manager who gave the umpires the most trouble. I've got to say that the late Freddie Hutchinson, who managed at St. Louis and in Cincinnati, was worse. Hutch was an absolutely wonderful person off the field, a man's man. Everybody respected him. He was so admired that immediately after his death many baseball people, including some sportswriters, got together and started a Fred Hutchinson Memorial Cancer Fund. Hundreds of thousands of dollars have been raised in his honor.

But he underwent some kind of metamorphosis when he was between the lines. He couldn't leave the umpires alone. And after the game was over, he could never leave it on the field. He played to win and never forgot a loss. Sometimes after an especially tough loss, he'd run amok in the clubhouse. He set a modern record for breaking light bulbs, chairs, tables, anything—a grown man driven to violence by a game.

He was the only man I ever challenged. I made two calls, on half-swings, one on Gil Hodges and another on Carl Furillo. Back-to-back. Hutchinson began bellowing, all the way from the dugout, and I unloaded him. The rule says you can't beef on a pitched ball. Then he came out to argue. I just couldn't get rid of him. He hung on like a burr.

"You're a big man out there," he said. "I'd like to punch you right in the mouth."

"Be my guest," I said. "I'll meet you after the game."

I was there, waiting, but he never showed.

Umpires have been punched and knocked down. I understand it happened more than a few times in the old days. John McGraw, the so-called great manager of the Giants, flattened Bill Byron—split his lip.

Byron, who had been a steamfitter, was a merry little guy and had a good voice. He was known as Lord Byron, the Singing Umpire, because sometimes he put his decisions into rhyme. To a player beefing about a third strike, Byron would chant:

> Let me tell you something, son,
> Before you get much older,
> You cannot hit the ball, my friend,
> With your bat upon your shoulder.

Byron switched from poetry to prose one day, after working a tumultuous Giant-Cincinnati game. Both managers were constantly beefing. Byron had the plate. After the game, McGraw started up with him again in the runway leading to the clubhouse. McGraw later contended that Byron insulted him in the runway and that's why he hit him.

A week later John Tener, then the president of the National League, fined McGraw $500 and suspended him for sixteen days. Then a very interesting thing happened which demonstrates that the press has twice as much power as an umpire—even an umpire who is punched in the mouth.

When the fine was announced, McGraw went into one of his characteristic rages. He told Sid Mercer, a famous New York sportswriter of the time, that Tener was a terrible league president, a no-good bum. McGraw called Tener every name in the book. Mercer wrote what McGraw said. And after the story came out, Tener was so furious that he slapped McGraw with an additional $1,000 fine.

I've never seen anybody punch an umpire, but Fred Hutchinson came the closest. Hutchinson went after Vinnie Smith, a very good umpire. It happened in Los Angeles, in the days when the Dodgers played at the Coliseum.

It was a play at second base. Men on first and second. The batter hits a grounder to the shortstop, who throws to the second baseman for the force. A routine double-play ball. But the runner, after sliding into the bag, grabbed the second baseman and prevented him from throwing to first. Vinnie called a double penalty. Two outs.

I can still see Hutchinson's face. He was so mad there were tears in his eyes. I thought he was going to punch Vinnie. I was working first base and ran between them. And what made this such an unusual situation was that off the field Hutchinson and Vinnie Smith were friends, super friends. They had been teammates in the minor leagues. Vinnie used to catch him. And two hours later they were friends again. We stayed at the Mayflower Hotel and after the game I saw Hutch and Vinnie sitting in the bar having a drink.

Hutchinson picked on everybody. I remember once he gave Lee Weyer a particularly hard time. At that time Weyer was only twenty-four, the youngest umpire in the history of the National League. Hutchinson came out on a close play at the plate and called Weyer a young punk.

"I might be young," Weyer told him. "But I'm going to run my ball games."

Hutchinson kicked dirt on the plate. It was Lee's first ejection. I don't think he ever had to unload him again.

Hutchinson's temper was monumental. Many of his players were afraid of him. There was one game in Milwaukee I'll never forget. The Reds were winning by two runs with two outs and the bases empty in the ninth. Joe Nuxhall, who is now a Cincinnati broadcaster, was pitching for the Reds. Nuxhall is famous because he was the youngest player to get in the big leagues. He came up during the war years, when he was fifteen. But the incident I'm referring to happened much later, when he was in the middle of his career.

Hutchinson was smiling, anticipating a victory. Why not? Two runs up and Nuxhall only has to get one more out and the game is over. But Nuxhall then gave up a single and the next guy hit one down to Roy McMillan, the Reds' great shortstop, and McMillan bobbled it. The tying run was now on base and up comes Eddie Mathews. Nuxhall hangs a 2–2 curve and Mathews, a great home-run hitter, takes it downtown. The Reds lose 3–2.

I thought Hutchinson was going to have a heart attack. He grabbed a bat and just stood there in the dugout. Poor Nuxhall didn't know what to do. He was afraid to come in off the mound. Finally Hutchinson took the bat and knocked out all the lights in the runway and then went into the clubhouse, screaming, "Where is that damned left-hander?"

Nuxhall was so frightened he didn't go to the dressing room. He walked right out into the street—in full uniform

—got into a cab, and went straight to the hotel.

Sometimes when I was on a long flight and had nothing to do, I'd make up two lists, a Bad Guy Club and a Good Guy Club. I'd list the players and managers entirely from a behavior standpoint, how they treated the umpires. It had nothing to do with their playing or managing ability.

Hutchinson was manager of the Bad Guy Club, with Durocher second, and Solly Hemus, Eddie Stanky, and Gene Mauch tied for third. Sparky Anderson, who had a great career at Cincinnati, was pretty high up there, too.

Stanky—they called him the Brat—was a clever little guy, but what a nuisance. One day Stanky bumped me. He stumbled and fell and got up, very embarrassed at having fallen down. But it was accidental. I knew he didn't mean to bump me. He just sort of bounced off my big chest. Even after getting up and dusting himself off he still continued to argue. With some of those guys it was an instinctive reaction. Blame the umpire. That's all they knew.

One night, when he was managing the Cardinals, a couple of tough calls went against him. He went out to change pitchers. I gave him plenty of time but he was dillydallying, so I went out to the mound. Finally he waved to the bullpen.

This was in the days when they first started using jeeps to bring the relief pitcher in from the bullpen. I said to Stanky, "Who's coming?"

He didn't answer. The rules say a manager has to tell you the name of a player as the player is coming into the game. A manager can be fined twenty-five dollars for an unannounced substitution.

Sometimes they say, "Can't you see? Are you that blind?"

I said to Stanky, a second time, "Who's coming in?"

He says, "Houdini."

"Okay, Eddie, but I'll tell you something. If Houdini doesn't get out of that jeep, you're done for the night."

Al Brazle got out and Mr. Stanky was gone. I unloaded him.

Durocher did that, too. One day in Chicago, Jim Hickman came to the plate as a pinch batter. I looked down toward the Cub dugout but I didn't see Durocher. I knew where he was. He was hiding in the runway.

Hickman was standing there, a very fine gentleman. I said, "Did Durocher send you up?"

"Yeah."

"Well, get in the box."

I signaled to the field announcer that Hickman was batting for so-and-so. What the hell, I'm not Christopher Columbus. I'm not about to go on a search party for Durocher. The PA man announces Hickman and wouldn't you know, Durocher comes out of hiding. I waited for him. I didn't meet him halfway. I let him use his little legs.

"I didn't tell you anything, Tom. Hickman isn't my hitter."

"I don't care if you told me or not. He's here. He's your hitter and he's in the ball game."

Durocher protested, but the league office threw it out. I always figured that as soon as a man took his position in the field, or in the batter's box, he was in the game.

Players don't go into a game on their own, though I think it happened once in Los Angeles. It was the sixth or seventh inning when I looked up and saw Wally Moon in left field, a defensive replacement. I gave his name to the announcer in the press box. Out came Walter Alston, the Dodger manager. "Tom, I didn't send him out there."

"Well, he's there and that's where he's going to be."

Maybe Walter didn't send him. Moon may just have been tired of sitting on the bench and figured it was time he got into a game. But it made no difference. Once he was in position he was in the game.

Joe Linsalata, a young umpire in the American League, lost his job in part because of an unannounced substitution. This was in the early sixties. Linsalata had a Yankee–Red Sox series in Boston. A pinch hitter came to the plate and Linsalata put him in the game. Later, Ralph Houk, who was then the Yankee manager, protested, insisting he didn't send him in. And damn if Houk didn't win the protest. Joe Cronin, the American League president, was in the stands and saw it happen. At the end of the year Linsalata was gone. The row with Houk was one of the reasons Cronin fired him.

Some managers are constantly reading the rule book, looking for loopholes. They carry it around like the Bible. Bobby Bragan was one of those guys. But Bragan was more of a comedian. He provided us with well-needed comic relief. For many years he was president of the minor leagues and a big and sincere supporter of the umpires. My, how they change! As a manager he wasn't among the best, but he did have a sense of humor. He participated in all kinds of shenanigans when he managed the Hollywood Stars in the old Pacific Coast League. Later he brought his bag of tricks to Pittsburgh.

One day, during a game in Milwaukee, there was a close call at second base. It was a hot, humid afternoon. Temperature in the nineties. Bragan got the bounce but a few minutes later sauntered back onto the field. In one hand he had a hot dog and in the other an orange drink, which he sipped through a straw. The umpires converged on him to see what the hell he wanted. The ball field isn't a dining room. But Bragan hadn't come out to argue. Instead he offered each of the umpires a bite of his hot dog and a sip of his soda. It was a famous photograph of the time: Bragan surrounded by umpires Frank Secory, Stan Landes, and Bill Baker. Bragan was fined $100 for his buffoonery and three days later the Pirates fired him.

I put Bragan on my Bad Guy Club, but I had him on mostly for laughs, and this club needed a court jester. There was nothing funny about the other guys.

Big, beefy Joe Adcock is my first baseman, a natural groaner. At second base I've got to go with Jackie Robinson, God rest his soul, a real beaut. Don Hoak, another scrapper, gets the nod at third. What a pain he was! There's only one candidate for short, Tim Foli, who is now with the Giants. He heads the list, absolutely on top, the worst I ever saw in the National League.

Foli had a reputation in the minors as a big umpire baiter, but most of us dismissed these reports. You can't go on what other people tell you. You find out for yourself. We found out. I think his problem is that he has to have an alibi every time he strikes out. So he tries to put the hat on us. He's a screamer and he throws everything—his bat, helmet, you name it. I'm surprised he doesn't throw his pants. Some of us thought he'd eventually calm down, but we were wrong.

My catcher is Smoky Burgess, who became very famous later in his career as a pinch hitter. The second-string catcher is Jerry Grote. He's mad at the world, wants everything. Another catcher who was always beefing was Randy Hundley of the Cubs. Hundley never used bad language like the rest of them. All he'd say was, "Jiminy Cricket, Tom, that was a good pitch." He'd give you that twenty to thirty times a game. Finally one day I called him aside before a game. I had the plate that day.

"Yes, Tom?" he said very respectfully.

"Do me a favor, will you?"

"Sure, Tom, anything."

"Well, stick that Jiminy Cricket up your ass."

He said he would, but he didn't. I guess it was too inbred.

I had four outfielders on my club, just in case one of 'em was hurt or in a slump and had to be benched. The regulars are Jim Pendleton, who played with Pittsburgh and Milwaukee; Cliff Johnson, when he was with Houston; and Ralph Garr, when he was at Atlanta.

Pendleton hit out of a crouch. He didn't like the inside half of the plate. He figured it wasn't part of the strike zone. And he had an awful habit of running to first base on 3–1 and 3–2 counts, as if he just took ball four. Johnson didn't say much, but every time I called a strike on him he turned around and looked at me like I had murdered somebody in his family. Johnson is with the Yankees now and doesn't do that anymore. We must have cured him. As for Ralph Garr, what a sweetheart. If he doesn't swing it's automatically a ball, because he insists he swings at every strike. I had to chase him twice in one week.

Frank Robinson, a really great player, was my fourth outfielder. He became the major leagues' first black manager. Off the field he had a lot of charm, like Fred Hutchinson. On the field he had a helluva time controlling himself, especially when he was a young player with Cincinnati. He was one of those guys who, after he's thrown out, is always struggling to get at the umpire, like he's going to mash him. One of the years that he won the Most Valuable Player Award, the umpires voted him the Sarah Bernhardt Award.

It's not only on the field that the players make trouble. Some of them like to sit in the dugout and yell. Don Newcombe was a classic. When he was pitching he never said a word. But when Newcombe was in the dugout he was always yelling at the umpires. I think he wanted to get chased. Bob Gibson was the same way. And Doug Rader— when he wasn't playing he was a terror. Lou Brock is another guy like that. When he's not playing he's always chirping.

Some young umpires have rabbit ears. They act too quickly in response to heckling. If the umpire turns too quickly and goes to the bench, he can stir up more trouble. All the players have got a reason to yell now and then, and the umpire's got to respond. Usually you can tell who's yelling from the bench. You could tell Jackie Robinson by his voice, and Durocher and Frank Robinson, too. Sometimes a player will holler, "I'm number forty-five! I'm the guy. It's me!" He wants to show his teammates that he's a big, brave man.

But an umpire has to be careful. Once, in 1946, the Red Sox were playing the White Sox in Boston. Red Jones, a famous umpire at the time, had the plate and reprimanded the Chicago pitcher, Joe Haynes, for throwing a beanball at Ted Williams.

Haynes was a quiet fellow, didn't have a reputation for trouble. Then Jones began hearing voices from the White Sox bench. Jones chased two players. The same voice kept coming from the dugout. Jones chased five more, and then, in frustration, ordered everybody off the bench. But the voice wasn't silenced. What Jones didn't know was that there was a ventriloquist sitting behind the White Sox dugout.

I had a similar experience one night in Philadelphia. Gene Mauch was managing the Phils and Don Hoak was their third baseman. Hoak had outsmarted me on a play the week before. The good umpire is supposed to forget yesterday's game, but I've got to confess I was still annoyed.

I had the plate and, from the beginning of the game, one of the Philly players got on my back and wouldn't get off. He'd yell, "Get the ball up." "Get the ball down." "Where's your Seeing Eye dog?" "Why don't you punch a hole in your mask?" Normally you can ignore some of this, but not when it continues and gets louder and louder. You have to take steps. By the seventh inning I had had enough. I had to take a shot at somebody and I figured it was Hoak. I could see him in the corner of the dugout. I knew he was making pretty good money. He could afford a fine. Besides, he was out with a bad leg. He wasn't even playing.

So I pointed toward the dugout and said, "Hoak, okay Hoak, you're out of there!"

Gene Mauch rushed to the plate. "Tom," he said, "what the hell are you doing? Why are you picking on my ballplayers? So far you've been working a pretty good game, not bad for you. You've only missed six or seven pitches so far."

"Don't play around with me," I said. "Get that donkey out of the dugout."

"Who you hollering at?" he asked.

"Don Hoak."

Mauch put his hands on his hips and pushed his face forward. "Let me tell you something," he said. "Hoak isn't in the dugout. He's in the bullpen."

Jesus. I looked at Gene. Down in the bullpen. Three hundred and eighty feet away. "Holy Moses," I said.

Gene said, "What're you going to do now?"

"Get him over here."

Gene waved to the bullpen. Hoak started in toward the plate. He thought he was going to pinch-hit. When he got to the plate Gene told him, "Gorman just put you out."

Don started raving and jumping up and down.

I said, "No more. Get out of here."

The next day I was walking through the runway when Hoak stopped me. "Tell me, Tom," he said, "how many times did I holler?"

"You hollered enough, and I don't want to hear any more."

"But answer me one thing, Tom. How the hell did you know I was hollering down in the bullpen?"

On my Good Guy Club there's only one candidate for first base and that's Gil Hodges, as good a man as you'll find in a long day's march. My second base combination is Bill Mazeroski of Pittsburgh and Pee Wee Reese of the Dodgers. Beautiful people. Ken Boyer, who is now managing the St. Louis Cardinals, is my third baseman. Roy Campanella is the catcher. The pitchers are Sandy Koufax and Don Drysdale.

In my outfield, I've got Stan Musial in left, Willie Mays in center, and Roberto Clemente in right. And now I've got a surprise. My team captain, who I can use at either first base or in left field, is Richie Allen. That's right, the Richie Allen who made a career out of controversy. In my time he led the league, or was among the leaders, in getting in and out of trouble.

We umpires never agreed with what Richie Allen did or didn't do in the clubhouse, or the way he was always disappearing. He must have been tough for a manager to handle. That he was traded four times in four years tells us that. But on the field, in his dealings with umpires, he was a great guy, one of the greatest ever to put a pair of shoes on.

I never saw Richie Allen argue. He and Bill Mazeroski. I never saw Mazeroski argue either. Maybe I should make them co-captains of my Good Guy Team. Two peas in a pod, though Richie, in a way, was a little more talkative. Richie was always asking about the family. And, please, don't be cynical and say he was friendly because he thought the umpires would give him a break. He didn't need help from anybody, not with that swing.

Every umpire in the National League has something good to say about Richie Allen. He was pleasant with everybody, not just with the veterans. Eddie Montague, a new umpire, told me that the first time Richie Allen saw him on the field Richie went over and introduced himself and wished him the best of luck.

And he was sincere. Many times, if there was a rhubarb on the field, Richie would take our side. I saw him pull Larry Bowa, the Philadelphia shortstop, out of an argument with Billy Williams. Billy had a close play at second base that went against the Phillies. Bowa screamed. Richie was playing first base. I don't know if Richie agreed with Billy's call or not. But he pushed Bowa away and said, "C'mon, let's play ball." This was a side of Richie Allen the fans never knew.

Richie always called me "Easy." I asked him why. He said it was because I made everything look easy.

Richie opened and closed his stormy career with the Phillies, and I'm glad he was on the field the day my retirement was announced. They put it on the scoreboard, that

I was retiring after twenty-five years in the league. The next inning Richie was on second base, got a double. All of a sudden he steals third. He beat the play with a good slide. Then he gets up and says, "Tom, I want to shake your hand."

"What for?"

"It's been a pleasure working with you. You've been a marvelous friend to me."

Roberto Clemente never argued either. He didn't need umpires. He just needed one pitch, the best right-field hitter I ever saw. Robby was strong all over. He hit so many line drives in the infield he's lucky he didn't kill anybody. He always complained about pains in his stomach. He'd come to the plate and I could see he was in pain and I'd say, "Robby, what's wrong?"

And he'd say, "Tom, I don't feel too good." But he didn't like to go to the doctor. He didn't believe in doctors.

Stan Musial was another champion. He didn't complain. One day in New York at the Polo Grounds, Stan hit three home runs in a row. The fourth time up Paul Pryor called him out on a half-swing. Stan didn't argue but Johnny Keane, his manager, came barreling out and gave Pryor all kinds of abuse. Pryor had to run him.

The next day Pryor was working third base. Musial at this time in his career was playing left field. Between innings, when Stan was running out to his position, he told Pryor, "That was a good call yesterday. The guy really fooled me on that pitch."

An umpire is supposed to be impartial, but I've got to admit there was a day when I was secretly rooting for Musial. I'll never forget it, a Sunday afternoon in St. Louis in September, when the Cardinals and the old Brooklyn Dodgers were fighting for the pennant.

The Dodgers were two runs up in the ninth inning. Jake Wade, a left-hander, was the Dodger pitcher and needed one out to end the game. The Cardinals were threatening

—bases loaded and Stan the Man coiled at the plate. Solly Hemus had Murry Dickson warming up just in case the game went into extra innings.

This was in the old ball park in St. Louis. There wasn't any bullpen. The pitchers warmed up adjacent to the left-field line. One of Dickson's warm-up pitches got away from the bull pen catcher and rolled into fair territory, at third base. I had the plate and Lee Ballanfant, a wonderful umpire, was working third. Lee saw this ball roll into fair territory and threw up his hands, signaling time.

The count was two balls and two strikes on Musial. Wade was at the top of his delivery but still had the ball in his hand. The pitch came in and Musial hit it over the right-field screen. You never saw such hollering and jubilation. The fans went wild. There were forty thousand people there and they were all Cardinal fans.

Charley Dressen, the Dodger manager, hurried to the plate. Dressen had seen Lee throw up his hands. Solly Hemus came to the plate from the other side, all smiles. He wanted to welcome Musial as he crossed the plate. I knew all hell was about to break loose, but I waited a few seconds for Lee Ballanfant to say something. Lee walked toward me. I met him halfway between third and home.

"Tommy, I called time," Lee said.

"I know. I saw you."

"We're going to be in for one hell of a battle."

"I know."

I walked back to Hemus, one of the great cheaters of my time. I said, "Solly, it doesn't count. Time was called."

Hemus groaned. You'd have thought I stuck a knife in his back.

Musial didn't know what happened. Neither did the fans. Musial was still circling the bases. Peanuts Lowrey was coaching at third and he started in on us. We chased Peanuts. We chased Hemus. Harry (the Cat) Brecheen got chased. We had to unload five or six Cardinal players. The police had to come on the field.

Musial came back to the plate and said, "Tom, what happened? It doesn't count, huh?"

I told him that Lee had called time before Wade had released the ball.

And Stan said, "Well, Tom, there's nothing you can do about it."

He got back in the box. Play resumed. Same situation. The count goes to three and two. I'm rooting like hell, the only time I ever rooted for a guy to get a hit.

"Hit one out, Stan!" I'm saying to myself.

And he hit a shot off the center-field screen, a triple. Three runs scored and the Cardinals won. I was so happy I could have kissed him. That's the only way we could have gotten out of there alive. But the point of the story is that the call didn't bother Stan. He accepted it. Most guys would have raised so much cain you would have had to chase them. Not Stan. He was a gentleman, in a class by himself.

My club has got to have managers, of course, and I picked two men above all the others: Walter Alston, who managed the Dodgers for twenty-three years, and Preston Gomez, who managed at San Diego and Houston. Preston didn't have much success, but that wasn't his fault. He had poor clubs. My coaches would be Casey Stengel, John McNamara, and Larry Doby.

I didn't see much of Doby when he was a player. He was in the American League, the junior circuit. But I got to know him when he was coaching for Gene Mauch at Montreal. Very fine gentleman, and he's from New Jersey, a neighbor of mine. Doby didn't beef much as a coach, but when he was managing the Chicago White Sox I noticed that he had a little ham in him. He could wind up a nuisance. I hope not, but I was watching the White Sox and Yankees on television one night and I saw where Doby, angry about a call, got down on his knees in a home-plate argument with Alan Clark. The White Sox had lost eight or nine in a row. I don't know, maybe Larry was just praying for a victory.

There are a lot of good guys who have managed. Danny Murtaugh, God rest his soul, cried and hollered but you had to like him. It was a tragedy that he had to die so young. Charlie Fox, when he managed the Giants, was a good one but he was too soft and his players took advantage of him. Bill Virdon is a fairly young guy, but already he has managed three clubs—the Pirates, Yankees, and Astros. He's another good one. He's tough, but he won't stick his head out of the dugout unless he's got a legitimate beef.

Clyde King, when he was a pitcher, was a real cutie. He'd quick-pitch, which was against the rules, and got so good at it that a lot of times he didn't get caught. But when Clyde became a manager he was on the up-and-up, a square guy. Danny Ozark is another good manager. So were Whitey Lockman, Stan Hack, and Red Schoendienst —fine men, on and off the field. They didn't cry wolf. When they had a beef you listened.

And you can't say too much about Casey Stengel. He slaughtered the king's English, but you always understood what he was saying. He communicated. He never got abusive, but he had one habit I had to call him on. He'd come out and argue, but instead of eventually walking away he'd walk in circles around us. Around, around, around, around. He made me dizzy. So one day I said, "Casey, next time around, you're gone. Stand still!"

When Casey managed the great Yankee teams, the Yankees and the old Brooklyn Dodgers would play two annual Milk Fund games, one in Yankee Stadium and the other in Brooklyn. I was at second base for the first game in 1952. The Dodgers were winning 5–3 in the fourth or fifth inning and Casey went out to talk to his pitcher, Johnny Kucks. I walked toward the mound and asked Casey what he was going to do.

"Why?" Casey asked. "You got someplace to go?"

I tried to hurry him along. The league office doesn't want the games to drag. Casey was stalling to give Don Larsen and Tommy Byrne time to warm up. "Come on, Case," I said, "let's go."

"All right, Tom, take your time. You're a National Leaguer, but don't get all excited."

Casey waved his left hand. That's a signal that the manager wants a left-handed pitcher to come in. I called for Tommy Byrne and he got about twenty feet behind second base when Casey turned around and saw him.

"Hey, lummox," Casey said to me. "I don't want him. I want Larsen."

"You put up your left hand," I said. "You got Tommy Byrne."

Casey appealed to Yogi Berra, his catcher. "Yogi, did I put up my left hand?"

"That's right," Yogi replied. "You put up your left hand."

"Yogi," Casey said, "who the hell you playing for?"

"Listen, Case," I told him. "All you've got to do is use Tommy Byrne for one hitter, let him retire one man, and then bring Larsen in and everything's all right."

Casey went back to the dugout. Byrne got the first hitter out, but Casey didn't move off the bench. The Yankees rallied and won the game.

The next day we moved to Brooklyn, to Ebbets Field. I had the plate. Casey walked up and said, "Good afternoon, Mr. Gorman."

"Good afternoon, Casey. And how are you?"

"Fine," he said. He kept up the chatter. It was getting late. Finally I had to ask him for his lineup card. He gave me his card and I looked it over. Umpires are always careful to inspect the lineup cards. But his was wrong and I told him so.

"What's the matter with it?" he asked, in all innocence.

"You forgot your pitcher. You've got no pitcher listed."

Casey laughed. He had set me up.

"Well, you did so good for us yesterday I was hoping you'd pick my pitcher again today."

And Gil Hodges—I have a regret about Gil Hodges that I'll never get over. He came out of Brooklyn and I came out of New York, and if a manager and umpire could have been close friends, we would have been. The first time he had a heart attack I was in Atlanta with him. He came up to the plate, not looking too good.

"Gil," I said, "what's the matter?" He said he was tired. They put him in the hospital that day, and he had the first attack the next day.

Later, he and I were in West Palm Beach, Florida, for a couple of exhibition games that were never played because the players went on strike. We ran into each other and he asked me what I was going to do. I told him I thought I'd drive home for a few days. He asked if I wanted to stay around and play some golf. I declined, I wanted to get home. And the next day he didn't play the usual eighteen holes. He played twenty-seven. Maybe it was too much for his heart. Maybe it would have been different if I'd stayed. God works in funny ways. This second attack took Gil Hodges away from us.

Hodges didn't argue much and, of course, neither did Walter Alston or Preston Gomez. We saw very little of Preston. It was a rare occasion when he argued, and when he did he was a gentleman. I've always thought that if I was a young player, just coming up, how wonderful it would be to play for him. He is a strong man, but has a quiet way about him. All the umpires admire him.

Once, I think it was when he was managing San Diego, his club was in a big slump. Preston was under fire, from both the fans and his front office. His general manager kept telling him he wasn't tough enough, that he should be out there arguing over every close call.

One time there was a close play at second base and

Preston came out, on the run. But first he told his shortstop, "Get back to your position. I'll handle this alone."

Then, when nobody else was within earshot, he said to Harry Wendelstedt, a very good umpire, "Look, Harry, I know you got the play right and I shouldn't be out here. But they're on my ass. They're telling me I'm not tough enough."

And so he went through all of the gestures. He went chin-to-chin, the whole routine, pretending he was madder than hell. Wendelstedt, being a good guy, helped him all he could. Harry shouted back and did a little gesturing of his own. And when it was over, Preston walked back to the dugout to a standing ovation. The fans loved it. I think that argument helped him finish out the season.

I don't want to give the impression that Preston never complained. He beefed. But he never gave you a cheap argument. He'd come out, state his case, and that was the end of it.

He did get thrown out at least once that I know of. This was when he was managing the Houston club. It was a game in Atlanta. There was a long drive to left field and Paul Runge, who was working third base, went out on the ball and called it a home run. But Runge wasn't sure about it and neither was John McSherry, who was working second base. Eddie Vargo, who had the plate, definitely saw the ball bounce over the fence. Since he was the only one who clearly saw the play, the home run was taken away from Houston and the batter was held to a ground-rule double. Preston was unloaded during the rhubarb.

But the strange thing was that Eddie Mathews, the Atlanta manager, didn't participate in the argument. Instead, Connie Ryan, one of the Atlanta coaches, came out. McSherry was curious about Mathews's absence. So the next day, at home plate, McSherry says to Mathews: "Where the hell were you when all the trouble was going on?"

Mathews laughed and said, "I wish you guys wouldn't have those tough plays when I'm in the bathroom."

Every team should have a front office and so my co-general managers would be Buzzie Bavasi, who is with the California Angels, and Gabe Paul, who is back with the Cleveland Indians. They're American Leaguers now, but they grew up in the National League. That's where I got to know them.

First impressions, as Jane Austen, the novelist, told us, are often erroneous. My first impression of Gabe Paul wasn't too good. This was almost a quarter of a century ago, when he was the general manager in Cincinnati. Once I was working with Frank Dascoli, and Gabe didn't like one of Frank's calls.

We had an icebox in our dressing room, so after the game we could have beer and sandwiches. The next day Gabe took the icebox away. He was like a little kid. He wouldn't let us have our beer. But he changed. He and Buzzie Bavasi are among the umpires' best friends. They even come down and say hello to us once in a while. Very few people do that.

Walter O'Malley, over the years, has also shown a rare consideration for the umpires. So I'll make him the owner of my Good Guy Club. Many people of my generation will never forgive him for moving the Dodgers from Brooklyn to Los Angeles but, in retrospect, it was a good thing. It opened up the West Coast to major-league baseball.

Walter was our man when the umpires went on strike in 1971. He went to bat for us—he and John Galbreath, the owner of the Pittsburgh Pirates. Horace Stoneham helped us, too. O'Malley said he didn't realize we were so under-paid and told the other owners we were right: we were entitled to more pay and better conditions. And whenever an umpire has to work a spring-training game in Vero Beach, Florida, Walter always sees that we're invited to lunch and that we can stay overnight at the Dodgers' camp if we want to. I never stayed, but at least he thinks of umpires as human beings.

Many times people ask me about Charlie Finley, the colorful owner of the Oakland Athletics. I've had only one adventure with him. This was in 1974, when I worked the Los Angeles–Oakland World Series. They played the first two games in Los Angeles, each team winning one, and then moved on to Oakland, where the games were supposed to start at five-thirty because of the Eastern television audience. One of the games in Oakland—I think it was the first—was delayed. Bowie Kuhn, the commissioner, came to the umpires' room to tell us why: "President Ford has nominated Rockefeller for vice-president and they're using the same cables that we're going to use to go back East."

You couldn't argue with that, but a little later Charlie knocked at the door and came in. "Where's Gorman?" he asked, though he knew me as well as I knew him, and I was sitting right by the door. "Charlie, here I am," I said.

He stood there with his green hat and his green suit on. "If it's not too much trouble for you, Tom," he said, "would you mind coming out and starting the game? I've got fifty-nine thousand people out there."

I told him I couldn't, and he asked why. "Because they're going to nominate Rockefeller for vice-president and they're going to use the same cable that we're using to go back East."

He stared at me for a minute. "He's using my cables," he said. "He's got a helluva lot of nerve."

"Charlie," I said, "why don't you go call him up?"

And he did.

He came back about ten minutes later. I asked him what happened.

Charlie frowned, in puzzlement and annoyance. "The President wouldn't talk to me," he said.

Basketball Team 1934
St. Augustine Boys School

1. The St. Augustine Boys School basketball team, 1934. I'm the one with the ball, third from right.

2. Warming up for the New York Giants, 1939.

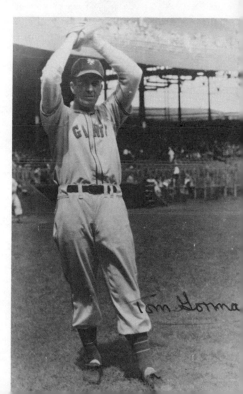

Tom Gorma

3. With my wife, Margie, soon after our wedding.

4. Bill Terry, my first manager, in a dispute with the legendary Bill Klem. *Wide World Photo*.

5. Casey Stengel giving me trouble after I sent his catcher, Chris Cannizzaro, to the showers. *UPI Photo*.

6. Willie Mays of the Mets and John Edwards of the Astros seem to be hanging on my every word.

7. Another ejection, this time Yogi Berra. *Wide World Photo.*

8. Cincinnati's Eddie Kasko (10), Joe Nuxhall (39), Ed Bailey (6), and manager Mayo Smith cluster around umpires Al Barlick (right) and Bill Jackowski to protest a play that gave the Pittsburgh Pirates the game-winning run. *Wide World Photo*.

9. Billy Williams, my partner for eleven years, making a call in a 1971 Cardinal–Giant game. Like all good umpires, Billy is taking a long look and isn't calling the play too quickly. The catcher is Dick Dietz of the Giants. The fellow on the bottom is Joe Torre, now manager of the New York Mets. *UPI Photo.*

10. Chris Pelekoudas has the last word with Leo Durocher. *Wide World Photo.*

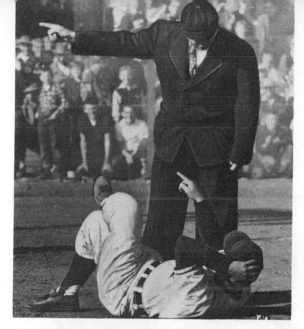

11. Bobby Bragan stages a "lie-in" to protest a ninth-inning decision by Emmett Ashford; standing alongside is umpire Al Mutart. *Wide World Photo.*

12. Ron Luciano in action. Though not all umpires approve of his theatrical style, Luciano is highly respected and in 1978 was named president of the Association of Major League Umpires. *UPI Photo.*

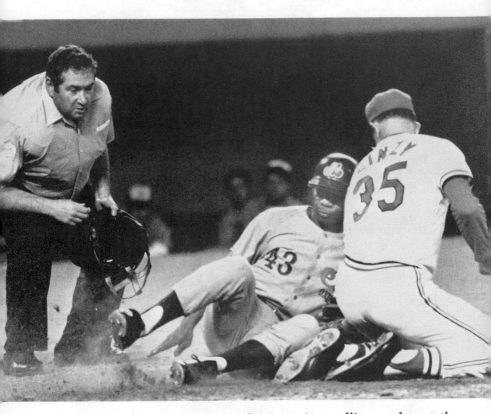

13. My old buddy Stan Landes in action, calling a play at the plate in a 1971 St. Louis–Montreal game. Pitcher Frank Linzy (35) makes the tag on Montreal's John Woods as he tries to score on a pitch that got away from catcher Ted Simmons. *UPI Photo*.

14. John McSherry, who chased a pigeon and Cincinnati manager Sparky Anderson in the same week. Here McSherry confronts the pigeon. *Wide World Photo*.

15. Babe Pinelli never missed a game during his twenty-two-year career, which ended with Don Larsen's 1956 perfect World Series game. Here Pinelli is with Larsen (left), and Yogi Berra. *Wide World Photo.*

16. With my kids. From left, Tommy, Brian, Patty Ellen, and Kevin. *Holland America Cruises by Flying Camera, Inc.*

17. Steve Yaeger of the Los Angeles Dodgers holds up the ball to show he still has it after a collision at the plate with Oakland third baseman Sal Bando. My son Tommy did a painting based on this photograph. *UPI Photo.*

If a player talks to me, I'll be civil, but it's not a good idea to try to be a player's pal. This pal-ship stuff doesn't work. But an umpire should be polite. You exchange pleasantries. You tell how the family is, if they ask, but it's not advisable to engage in lengthy dialogues.

Some players are great talkers. Outfielder Rick Monday of the Los Angeles Dodgers is always talking to the umpires. Some pitchers ask us how they're doing, whether they're better or worse than before. Or how their curve or slider is breaking. I don't tell them how to pitch, but I do answer their questions.

I had the plate for three or four games when Jerry

Koosman of the Mets was pitching, a nice fellow. One night in San Francisco he couldn't get anybody out. "Gee, Tom," he said, "what am I doing wrong?" And I said, "Well, this is a tough park." That's a proper answer in that situation. I'm an umpire, not a pitching coach.

Another big talker is Steve Yaeger, the Los Angeles catcher. He's not trying to distract the umpire or the batter, but sometimes you have to tell him, "Knock it off." You need total concentration. We call about three hundred pitches a game and we have to be right on every one of them. We don't want distractions.

Yogi Berra was another big talker. He caught in the American League, but I had the plate in the World Series when the Yankees played Milwaukee. He spouted an endless line of chatter. He was trying to distract the hitters. He'd ask how they were, what they planned after the season, what was new.

Once Yogi reminded Hank Aaron to hold the label on the bat straight up, or he'd break it. Hank said, "Hey, Yogi, I'm up here to hit, not to read."

Yogi was an exception to my rule about being civil. Every time he came to bat he'd say, "Hello, Tom, how's the family?"

Finally, I said, "They died last night. Get in there and hit."

Sometimes it works the other way around. Ron Luciano of the American League is unusually talkative for an umpire. When Carl Yastrzemski, the Boston Red Sox star, came to the plate in an important pennant-race game in 1974, he didn't want to be distracted by Luciano's usual idle chatter.

So as he stepped into the batter's box, Yaz said to Luciano: "I'm fine, my wife's fine, the kids are all fine. It's a nice day. Let me hit in peace."

Tom Haller, a star catcher who used to play with the Giants and the Dodgers, was more subtle with Bruce

Froemming, one of the younger National League umpires. This was in 1971, when Haller was with the Dodgers, and Froemming, after a long minor-league career, was in his first major-league season.

Haller, by this time, was in his eleventh big-league season, a very good catcher. In addition, he also knew something about umpires. His brother Bill has been an outstanding American League umpire for many years.

For five or six innings, Haller asked Froemming about every close pitch, not necessarily challenging him, but testing his judgment. Finally he popped the question.

"Bruce, what's your last name?"

"Froemming."

"Spell it," said Haller.

"F-R-O-E-M-M-I-N-G."

"That's with one *I?*"

"Yep," Froemming replied.

"That's exactly how you've been calling the game all night."

I suppose it's natural for catchers to be talkers. It's such a tight, cozy little group there at home plate. It invites talk. An outfielder can't talk to anybody, but a catcher's got a captive audience.

I recall an incident with Joe Garagiola, who is now a big television star. This happened when Garagiola was catching for St. Louis. We were late because our train was delayed. I hurried out to the field and forgot my mask. I couldn't work without a mask and I didn't want to ask the bat boy to get it for me. The players would hear and they'd say, "You'd forget your head if it wasn't tied on your shoulders." The players wait for spots like that.

Joe's mask was lying there before me, asking for it. I picked it up and put it under my arm. He was warming up the pitcher, and in a few minutes I said, "Let's go, we're almost late."

Garagiola looked all around, and said, "Gee, I must have

forgotten my mask. How could I do a thing like that?" He got another mask. I worked the whole nine innings with his mask. After the last out I thanked him, and handed it to him. "You know, Tom," he said, "I thought I was going out of my mind. I knew I brought a mask out here. But I didn't know what happened to the son-of-a-gun."

Hank Aaron was one of the quiet ones. He was always pleasant, but he didn't say much. When he broke Babe Ruth's home-run record there was a big celebration, and it was richly deserved. Finally the pressure was off. The weekend after the great day, there was a doubleheader in Atlanta that almost nobody attended. I was behind the plate for the second game. It got to be late—five or six o'clock—and Aaron came to bat. The pitcher worked the count to 2–2, and then threw a pitch right above the knees, on the outside corner. Nobody could hit a pitch like that one. *Nobody.* And so I yelled, "Strike three!" The next thing I knew the ball was sailing into the seats.

Aaron trotted around the bases and the catcher turned to me. "Tom," he said, "what the hell are you doing?"

"I'm practicing," I said.

It's not uncommon to run into the ballplayers during the winter, but it's never a good idea to try to become pals. You should, of course, be pleasant when you meet at a banquet. No harm in being pleasant. It's good for the soul. But sooner or later all umpires learn it's best to keep their distance.

Usually they make this discovery early in their careers. Bruce Froemming tells about the time when he was in the low minors, in the Northwest League, and made the mistake of playing a round of golf with a pitcher.

The pitcher heard Froemming was a good golfer and so they went out one afternoon and played eighteen holes. Two nights later Bruce had the plate when this guy was pitching. It was chaotic. The pitcher challenged him on every call and Bruce, in exasperation, had to unload him. And when he was ejected, the pitcher said, "You can forget about ever playing golf with me again." Froemming was delighted.

There are times when it's tempting to have dinner with a player, particularly if you've known the player before you came into the league. Bob Engel of the National League staff had known John Callison ever since Johnny was a kid. They lived across the street from each other in Bakersfield, California.

Callison was a very good player with the Phillies, a strong hitter, and one day, in Philadelphia, Callison invited Engel to his home for a barbecue dinner, after a Saturday-afternoon game.

"John, I'd really like to go," Engel told him. "But it's not a good idea. I'll be partaking of your hospitality and tomorrow I may have to call you out on strikes."

Callison didn't push it. He understood.

It isn't advisable to have a personal relationship with a player. I remember what happened to Lon Warneke, a very fine gentleman who was a famous pitcher with the Cubs. When he was finished playing, Lon turned to umpiring. I worked with him on the same crew for a full season.

Maybe Lon figured that because he had been a great pitcher the players would have more respect for him. Besides, he was their friend, or at least had been. It bothered him when he had to chase ballplayers he knew. Once, in Chicago, he got into a big rhubarb with Phil Cavarretta, who had been his manager with the Cubs. Lon chased him and in the cab on the way back to the hotel Lon said, "Tom, did you hear the language he used at me?"

I said, "You did the right thing, Lon."

But Lon could never get over it, and I'm sure that's one of the reasons he quit. He was in the league two years.

Ed Walsh, another famous Chicago pitcher, also tried umpiring. Walsh had been the toast of Chicago as a star with the White Sox. Many of his pitching records still stand. He had a pleasant personality and was well liked throughout the American League.

When the life had gone out of his arm, Ban Johnson, who was then the president of the American League, was eager to keep Walsh in baseball. Walsh agreed to become an umpire and for the last few months of the 1922 season was turned over to Billy Evans, at that time a veteran of the staff. Walsh did well, but he quit at the end of the season. Evans was puzzled and asked him why.

"It's a strange business, Billy," Walsh said. "All jeers and no cheers. You can have it!"

Ten, twelve years later the same thing happened to Firpo Marberry, another famous pitcher who gained his greatest fame as a reliefer with the old Washington Senators. Marberry was a handsome fellow and very popular. But he couldn't make the psychological adjustment. He had to make decisions against old teammates. Suddenly he found himself assailed and abused by old clubhouse friends. He was hurt and bewildered. He, too, quit at the end of the season. He was the last umpire to come into the big leagues without minor-league experience.

An umpire isn't even safe in church. One Sunday, in Milwaukee, I went to mass with Augie Donatelli and Artie Gore, two of my partners. Sometimes Johnny Logan, who was then the Milwaukee shortstop, went to the same church on Wisconsin Avenue.

The monsignor was a baseball nut. I don't know if we had his real name, but we always called him Father John. The three of us went to communion and after the mass we were standing on the steps, talking to Father John, when out came Logan.

So Father said to Logan, "How nice to see you. Do you see my three umpires? They all went to mass and hit the rail. How about you?"

And Logan said, "Father, they need it."

ome people say umpires are similar to Supreme Court justices. It's a flattering comparison but not accurate. We don't sit in high-backed chairs making weighty judgments. We just call balls and strikes. And we don't sit on cases for months or years at a time.

About ten or fifteen years ago a fellow sent me a book about the inner workings of the Supreme Court. I still have it—*Gideon's Trumpet.* It follows a particular case from beginning to end. What I remember most is the book took 238 pages to explain how the justices reached their decision. That's a long time to find out whether the guy is safe or out.

In baseball we've got to decide in a split second, and once we hand down a ruling, that's it. Our decisions can't be reversed by another generation of umpires, twenty or thirty years later. There is no appeal. We've got to be right the first time.

One of the umpiring schools made a statistical study and estimated that an umpire in one nine-inning game:

Calls 288 balls and strikes.
Calls 64 players safe or out (all bases).
Calls 56 players safe or out (first base).
Gets hit by a hit, or hit by a pitched ball once.

Think about that. An infielder must have thirty-two consecutive errorless games to have as many opportunities to make a mistake as an umpire in one game of calling balls and strikes.

And a batter must hit safely every time he is at bat in fifteen games to be as good as the umpire is expected to be in his calls at first base for one game.

Obviously, we can't get every call right, but I'd have to say, and as the instant replay seems to indicate, we're like Ivory soap, 99.44 percent pure. And I believe in the famous remark made by Bill Klem, the patron saint of umpires, who according to the legend said, "I never missed one in my heart."

Actually, Klem didn't say it quite that way. But that's the way it came out in the wash. What he said was, "I never missed one of those in my life." But Mr. Klem admitted he was delighted with the change. It gave him a million dollars' worth of publicity and singled him out above all the other men in our profession.

Klem, in his biography, said it all stemmed from a controversial play he had in 1912. The Cubs were playing John McGraw's Giants in the Polo Grounds and in the eighth inning a Giant hitter slapped one against the scoreboard in left field. The scoreboard spanned both foul and fair territory. The foul line stopped at the base of the scoreboard and continued upward from the top of the scoreboard. But there was no line on the scoreboard itself.

Klem followed the flight of the ball. When it struck the scoreboard he yelled, "Foul."

McGraw, of course, insisted it should have been a home run. McGraw was the number-one umpire-baiter of his day. Klem was his favorite target; McGraw was always at his throat. More than once he tried to get Klem fired.

It so happened that the Polo Grounds had been rebuilt after a fire the year before. The scoreboard was new and made of metal. Two days after the incident, Jim Foster, the architect who had rebuilt the Polo Grounds, went to see Klem.

"Wilyum," Foster said, "McGraw made me get out plumb lines and climb up on that scoreboard to find the dent the ball had put in it. Then I measured it, and you know that ball was foul by three inches?"

"You're not telling me a thing, Mr. Foster," Klem roared. "I never missed one OF THOSE in my life."

What Klem meant was that it was a simple play. Like all of us, when the ball is in flight, Klem straddled the foul line. Perfect position. Klem saw the ball curve to the left and ruled it a foul ball. I've got to go with Klem.

Foster told McGraw what Klem had said, but in relaying the statement Foster edited it and had Klem saying, "I never missed one in my life." Later, it underwent another change and today Klem is known for having said, "I never missed one in my heart."

I never worked with Klem. He retired in 1940, about ten years before I got into the National League. But I saw him work once in Florida, in 1946, when I was a player with the Giants. We were in Miami for an exhibition. At that time it was a small field. We knew Klem was in the stands, sitting along the railing.

I went over and said hello to him. I had heard so much about him, I wanted to meet him. He said, "Nice to meet you, kid. Good luck to you."

One of the umpires didn't show up that day, so they brought Klem out of the stands. He worked third base, in a sweater. He had been suffering from some illness and—please, no jokes about this—at that time he only had one eye. I think he lost the eye because of diabetes.

I remember Ernie Lombardi, the big catcher, yelling to Klem, "Hey, Bill, I thought I got rid of you a long time ago. Now you've come back to haunt us."

Klem wasn't very big. He was a feisty little guy. Later, I heard he didn't get along with too many of his fellow umpires, that he was tough to work with, that he was never wrong, but was quick to tell somebody else that he was wrong. You know, stuff like, "You kicked that, kid."

An umpire should never show up his partners. That's rule Number One in the Umpires' Manual. I'm not saying that if you're working with a younger umpire you should always tell him he made the right call, even when he's wrong. I don't believe in that either. He should learn from his mistakes, and you're doing him an injustice if you don't tell him the truth.

Rule Number Two is that a league president should always support his umpires—at least publicly. There are times when a league president may be correct in fining an umpire. Most fans don't know it, but umpires occasionally are fined. But when this happens, the league shouldn't make a public announcement about it. The umpire, in his public image, must be regarded as infallible. If you chip away at his infallibility, you're destroying his effectiveness as an umpire.

In the early 1950s, Warren Giles, then the president of the National League, made such a mistake. Giles was at a game in Cincinnati, which at that time was the league headquarters. Umpire Scotty Robb had the plate and got into a stomach-pushing contest with Eddie Stanky, the Cardinal manager.

Robb had called Solly Hemus out on strikes. An argument followed. Stanky bustled up to Robb and pushed his little tummy at him. Robb, who was about twice the size of Stanky, reacted like a man who was tired of being shoved around. He pushed back, harder. The next day Giles fined Hemus twenty-five dollars for his part in the incident, and took fifty dollars from Stanky. Then Giles announced he had fined Robb "a sizable amount, much larger than the combined fines of the players involved." It was believed to be $200.

Giles's reaction, in a sense, was proper. He didn't want the players pushing his umpires around, but he didn't want his umpires pushing the players either. What Giles didn't foresee was that the larger fine, and all the publicity, came to be a constant embarrassment to Robb. The umpire-baiters picked up on it. Robb thought it would never stop. He also believed Giles had been unfair. Soon thereafter, Robb quit and went into the American League.

An umpire has to have respect from the players and the league office, and from his fellow umpires. It always bothers me when umpires fight among themselves. I don't know why this should be, but I've seen a lot of jealousy in our profession, and it goes way back. It almost seems to be a tradition.

Klem, for example, feuded with other umpires. Klem and Hank O'Day barely spoke to each other. I didn't realize this until I read that Klem knocked O'Day for calling Fred Merkle out at second base in the famous 1908 game between the Giants and the Cubs. Klem said O'Day made a bad call, that Merkle should not have been called out for not touching second. I couldn't believe Klem said that. Merkle was definitely out, according to the rules. But Klem insisted that, on that particular play, the rules should not have been enforced. Later, I mentioned this to one of the older umpires. "How could the great Bill Klem say that?" I asked. And this umpire told me Klem didn't like O'Day and was always criticizing him.

The Merkle play—it's known in baseball history as "Merkle's Boner"—occurred in the heat of the pennant race. Some background information is necessary to fully understand what happened. On September 4, the Cubs were in Pittsburgh. The Pirates won the game with two outs in the ninth inning when a Pittsburgh runner scored from third base on a clean single to the outfield by Chief Wilson. However, another Pittsburgh runner on first base, Warren Gill, did not run to second base. Gill stopped halfway between first and second and ran off the field.

Johnny Evers, a big umpire-baiter—he was known as the Crab, the Tim Foli of his day—called for the ball and stepped on second base for a force-out on Gill. Evers then protested to O'Day, who was umpiring alone that day, that the run didn't count, the reason being that Chief Wilson, the batter, can't be safe at first until the preceding runner, Gill, had advanced to the next base. It's a simple and elemental rule.

O'Day agreed that Evers's interpretation was correct but said he was so occupied watching the batter and the runner at third, he didn't notice whether or not Gill had touched second before leaving the field. O'Day didn't allow Evers's protest but said if the play came up again he would be watching for it and call it according to the rules.

The same play did come up again, less than three weeks later, on September 23, when the Giants were playing the Cubs in the Polo Grounds. The Giants were leading the league and the Cubs were in second place, one game back. The famous Christy Mathewson was pitching for the Giants against Jack Pfiester.

The score was tied 1–1, Giants batting, two outs, and two men on—Moose McCormick was on at third and Merkle on at first. Al Bridewell singled to center and McCormick came running home. But Merkle, who was then in his second major-league season, didn't run all the way to second and instead ran into the clubhouse, believing the game was over.

Again, Evers called for the ball and stepped on second. O'Day ruled the run did not count. By this time most of the players had gone to the clubhouse. The crowd was on the field. It was impossible to go into extra innings. O'Day ruled the game a 1–1 tie.

The Cubs and Giants finished their regular schedule in a tie, so the game had to be replayed. The Cubs won this special playoff game and what I find interesting is that Klem, not O'Day, had the plate for the playoff. O'Day wasn't assigned to the game. And after the game, Klem told reporters: "I never umpired a better game."

But the point to remember is that O'Day made the correct decision. Klem was wrong in criticizing him. Klem contended that "any judge will tell you that it is the intent of the law which counts, not the phraseology." He said the intent of the rule applied only to infield grounders and not to cleanly hit drives to the outfield that makes a force impossible unless the runner at first drops dead. "And custom, another strong factor in all law, had long established the right of a man to leave the field when there was no reasonable doubt that the game was over."

I have news for Mr. Klem: He was wrong. If the rule is in the book, the umpire must follow the rule. If it's a poor rule the Rules Committee should take it out of the book. The umpire doesn't make the rules, but it's his job to enforce them.

It pains me when I see umpires fighting amongst each other. My idea is that we're all in the major leagues. There's no higher place to go. But some of the younger guys, after two or three years, start telling the old-timers what to do. It shouldn't be like that. We all have the same job. I always emphasized to my crew that whatever happens between the four of us, we must always stay together. I don't want to hear one umpire knocking another. Sometimes we act like a bunch of chorus girls.

In the minor leagues you work with one guy—two-man teams. There's more devotion between the umpires that way. The two get along like brothers. They go everywhere together. They drive together. Then you come to the big leagues and expect the same thing and it's not there.

There have been some fistfights between umpires. I once saw Jocko Conlan and Artie Gore go at it. Shag Crawford went at it with Artie Gore another time. They had a couple beers in them. Larry Goetz and I had it out in the dressing room in Pittsburgh. He did something I didn't like and then he called me a busher.

Larry called me a busher because I didn't rub the balls up. Larry came into the dressing room about fifteen minutes before the game. I don't know if he was used to some-one else rubbing the balls. The fellow who has the plate is supposed to rub the balls himself. He took the balls out of the sack and said, "Hey, busher, how come you don't have the balls rubbed up?"

"Don't call me busher," I said, and that was the start of it.

Larry and I never got along. After he retired he had a nervous breakdown and was in the hospital in Cincinnati. I went to see him and spent a couple of hours with him talking about baseball. He seemed glad to see me. A month later I came back to Cincinnati. He was out of the hospital and sitting up in the press box with the newspapermen, up in the coop. He walked right by me and never said hello. But he was a very good umpire. He made himself a good umpire. He was devoted to the game.

But Larry always wanted everything his way. Once, it wasn't his turn to work the World Series. He had been assigned to the Series a few years before, but he called Mr. Giles anyway and asked him if he could work. Mr. Giles turned him down. I can still hear Goetz saying, "Well, why don't you give me the foul lines so I can be out there anyway." Larry was being unfair. He didn't care about the younger umpires.

Sometimes Jocko Conlan was a problem, too. Jocko was a good umpire, but he thought everybody should work the way he did, that his style was the best. I broke in with Al Barlick, one of the great umpires, and we're friends, but sometimes I think Al wasn't happy unless he was knocking someone. I've heard some of the stories he's told about me and I wonder what's the matter with him. I don't know what it is. For some reason or other, he's always carrying a chip on his shoulder.

I always had a lot of respect for Babe Pinelli. Yet some of the other umpires didn't like him. Dusty Boggess was another outstanding umpire. He had an autographed baseball signed by all the umpires he ever worked with down through the years. And he took that autographed ball to the grave with him. He had it specified in his will.

have always empha-
sized that umpires should get along with each other, but
the fact that we do have some intramural squabbles doesn't
surprise Jerry Dale, who says that umpires are strong-
willed men and, because of this, some friction is inevitable.

Jerry is a veteran National League umpire and, so far
as I know, is the only person who has done a character
study, complete with a statistical analysis, of the personality of umpires at the amateur and major-league levels. He
worked on it for a long time and reached some interesting
conclusions.

Jerry began umpiring in 1963 and has been in the National League for almost ten years. He has been, and I'm

sure still is, very dedicated, both to umpiring and to completing his education. He has a wonderful tenacity about him. It took him fourteen years going to school, during the off-season, to get his bachelor's and master's degrees.

He wrote up his study of umpires as a master's thesis at California Poly in Pomona. You can say Jerry Dale put us under glass to find out what makes us tick. For purposes of comparison, 103 students at the Al Somers Umpiring School had filled out lengthy questionnaires; the same questionnaires were sent to all of the forty-eight major-league umpires, though only twenty-nine of the big-league umpires responded.

The study revealed what Jerry and a lot of us always suspected—umpires, as a group, are aggressive, assertive, argumentative, hard-headed, extroverted, and loquacious, and we would get high marks in handling people in difficult and pressure situations. These characteristics didn't show up, at least not beyond the norm, in the student umpires, however, leading to the obvious conclusion that there is a personality change as an umpire rises in his profession. The professional umpire learns early that, to survive, he can't stay in his cozy cocoon. He must be forceful and grow a thick skin.

I'm no psychologist, but I've seen enough and been around long enough to know this is true. In his study, Jerry repeatedly uses the word *adaptable.* He says umpires are much more adaptable than most people and that this ability to adjust is a necessity. A strong and decisive hand is needed to successfully deal with the daily arguments and pressures. He also said umpires are absolute realists. The fans have a romantic view of the players, which is fine. They wouldn't pay to see a ball game if they didn't regard the players as heroes. But the umpires see a side of the players the fans never see—the worst.

I don't want to shatter anyone's illusions, but you'd be amazed at the language a nineteen-year-old shortstop can throw at us. And that kid pitcher, the one with the dimples, can be an awful pain in the ass. I remember one of these fuzzy-faced kids, a pinup boy, a rookie of the year. He badgered me all night because I didn't call enough strikes. And this was in his second major-league start. I told him, "Kid, if it's a strike, you'll get it. And if it isn't, you won't." He never heard me. He's now a thirty-six-year-old veteran, graying at the temples. And still complaining. But his image with the fans is great: they think he's Jack Armstrong, the all-American boy.

I agree with Jerry that most of the umpires do seem to have the characteristics he mentioned, though in varying degrees. But I also pointed out to him that there were some umpires who don't conform to this pattern: men like Ed Sudol and Nick Colosi and Andy Olsen. They keep a low profile, particularly Sudol, who recently retired after a long and distinguished career.

Jerry had an interesting answer. He insisted that most umpires, Sudol included, have a dual personality. He said, and he was correct, that Sudol had an unusually flamboyant manner when he worked the plate. On the field, Sudol was aggressive and an extrovert. Off the field he was considerably more quiet. Jerry also contends that the umpires, during off-season, when they are home with their families, aren't overly forceful or garrulous.

Many years ago the *Sporting News* published one of those polls on umpires, listing different categories: best on balls and strikes; best on the bases; best dressed; toughest; loudest voice; and so on. They also had a category for "most diplomatic." Augie Donatelli, now retired and a good friend of mine—we worked together for years—was chosen as the number-one umpire in "diplomacy."

Augie, who had been a B-17 tail gunner during World War II, called the editor of the *Sporting News* and raised the roof. Augie took a dictionary with him into the telephone booth and read the definition of the word *diplomat:*

"One who is versed in or makes a business of diplomacy; a diplomatist; characterized by artful dealings, tact, and cleverness in avoiding blunders; politic in conduct; art of conducting negotiations between nations."

"You've got the wrong guy," Donatelli said. "Look at my record. I lead the league in ejections. Nobody can unload them as fast as I can."

No umpire wants to lead the league in ejections. Donatelli didn't want to either. But he didn't know what else to say and he had a legitimate beef. The last thing he wanted was to be pictured as a striped-pants diplomat who sits down with the manager and players for seventh-inning tea.

But a certain amount of diplomacy is essential on our job. If it's possible to smooth things out, fine, handle the situation accordingly. I do think some of the younger umpires sometimes have a quick thumb. But there's a reason for that, too. The managers and players take more liberties with a new umpire. They test him out to see how far they can go, how much he'll take. But once they start using abusive and obscene language, it's got to be "Good-bye, Charlie, see you tomorrow."

Most fans believe the best umpire—the best officials in any sport—are those they don't see, that the good umpire is invisible. This is a popular misconception. If you don't notice an umpire, it's for one reason. It was an easy game and there were no tough calls.

Sometimes, though, people become so engrossed in a game they see nobody but the players, which I think is fine. This happened to John McSherry's mother, a die-hard Met fan. John is one of the younger umpires in the National League, a very fine umpire. He grew up in New York, and whenever he works the Mets, his mother usually comes to the game. He was very excited this particular day because he would be working the plate, his first plate job in New York.

John had told his mother, when he was a kid, that someday he'd be a major-league umpire and he'd be sure she had a box seat right behind the plate so she could see him work.

As he said he would, he got his mother a choice box seat. It was a big game, a sellout that went eleven innings, with a rain delay. A long game.

The Mets won on a close play at the plate. Bud Harrelson scored the winning run. After the game, John's mother met him outside the umpires' dressing room. John introduced her to his partners and then said, "Well, Mom, what'd you think?"

She looked at him and said, "John, I never thought we'd get that run."

He said, "The run? What about me?"

"Oh," she said, "you did fine, too, son."

Bill Kunkel, an American League umpire, had a similar experience. Bill and I worked the 1974 World Series together. The Oakland A's beat the Los Angeles Dodgers in five games. As the senior man, I had the plate in the first game. Bill had the plate in the second game. This second game was the only game the A's didn't use Rollie Fingers, their star reliefer.

The next spring, at the start of the season, Bill was working an Oakland game. Bill has an old battered cap which he treasures. He's been wearing it for years. Fingers noticed his old cap and said to Kunkel, "Hey, Bill, isn't it about time you worked the Series and got a new cap?"

Kunkel was amazed and told him, "What do you mean? I worked the Series last year."

Billy Martin, the in-again, out-again manager of the New York Yankees, heard this story and seized upon it as an example of an umpire working a perfect Series. According to Martin's reasoning, Kunkel must have called every play right. Otherwise, Fingers would have noticed him.

But I can assure you of this: Fingers wouldn't have forgotten if Bill had been behind the plate in any of the other four games. A pitcher doesn't forget the umpire who is at the plate when he is pitching. It was a coincidence that the one game Fingers didn't get into, the second game, was when Kunkel had the plate.

Being noticed, or not noticed, is not an indication of an umpire's effectiveness. I always go back to Al Barlick, one of the great umpires of my time. Umpiring was like a religion to Barlick. From the first ball or strike, you knew Barlick was in the ball park. Barlick had that tremendous booming voice. You could hear him in the next county.

There are a few umpires, of course, who put on a show. There's no way you can possibly miss Ron Luciano, who works in the American League. Luciano is a big fellow, a former football player, and a character in his own right. Luciano dances on the field, shakes hands with the players and pats 'em on the rear.

Emmett Ashford also puts on a show. A lot of people criticize Ashford and Luciano, but their antics never bothered me and the fans certainly enjoy them. What I consider more important is that they're good umpires. Luciano is also very outspoken off the field. He's made many disparaging remarks about some of the American League managers. I'm sure the league office would like to put a muzzle on him, but he keeps talking, and when he talks he tells the truth. I say more power to him.

There have been many colorful umpires. The fans don't come to the ball park to see the umpires, they come to watch the players. But the late Ed Danforth, who was the sports editor and columnist for the *Atlanta Journal,* always insisted that Harry "Steamboat" Johnson was a genuine gate attraction. Steamboat was an umpire for forty years, almost all of them in the minor leagues. He became an institution in the Southern League. He had a restaurant in Memphis, his hometown, and was one of the few umpires to write his autobiography. It's called *Standing the Gaff.* He estimated he made about one million decisions and had approximately four thousand bottles thrown at him, about twenty of which hit him. Steamboat got his nickname because he had a foghorn voice.

Modesty does not prevent me from saying I had a pretty good voice myself. A baritone. I don't think I could sing at the Metropolitan Opera, but I was an altar boy at St. Augustine in the Bronx, now called Cathedral of the Bronx. But in my time, the fellow with the strongest voice was Barlick. And he could keep it up for nine innings.

Dutch Rennert, one of the National League's good young umpires, is maintaining the tradition. Dutch isn't very big in size—only about five feet seven inches—but he can bellow. He worked at it, too. Dutch is from Oshkosh, Wisconsin. Used to deliver mail up there. He patterned himself after two Big Ten basketball officials, Jim Enright and Bud Lowell, both of whom have strong voices. Off the field, Dutch Rennert has a quiet manner, very soft-spoken. But you can't go to sleep when Dutch is working the plate. The only catcher who gave Dutch a hard time was Jerry Grote when he was with the Mets. Grote used to catch with cotton in his ears.

speak a lot at banquets during the winter, and one night in Boston a lady asked me a question that had been on her mind for several years. She was a big Red Sox rooter, and I could tell by the way she spoke she was sympatico with umpires. Maybe she had a boyfriend who was a man in blue, or who liked to wear dark blue suits. I don't know. She asked what we do when we have to go to the bathroom. A lot of people ask about that.

Between the two games in a doubleheader there's no problem because we go to our dressing room and have twenty minutes between games. During single games, extra-inning games, marathons, etc., we use the bathrooms in each dugout while the teams are changing sides. Usually nobody even notices you're gone, except for your partners.

In Houston one night, Paul Pryor had to make an emergency call. Paul rushed into the dugout, on the double, zipped his pants up real quick, and started to go out. But the Houston players, led by the late Don Wilson, a very good pitcher, locked him in. Pryor banged on the door.

"Let me out! Let me out!"

Paul was working first base, and when he didn't get back in time his partners assumed he was sick and continued the game. But the Houston players relented and unlocked the door. Paul missed only a few pitches.

Most umpires are big coffee drinkers, myself included, but I never drink anything before a game. Eddie Sudol always tried to get me to take salt tablets, but I didn't take them either. They made me nauseated. When it's hot, temperature in the nineties, you can lose as much as thirteen to fifteen pounds working the plate.

There's one thing about the new parks that not many people seem to notice. The playing fields, most of them, are below ground level. It's like being in a pit. There's not much air circulating down there. And the artificial turf adds to the discomfort. It's like standing barefooted in a steam bath. The heat comes right through your shoes. By the fifth inning your puppies are boiling. The players go into their dugouts between innings and can sit down and cool off. But we have to stay out there. That's why a lot of us move around. Between innings, I always tried to get to the dirt part of the infield. The ground isn't as hot.

We have to be careful about what and when we eat. I never ate a big meal before the game. It makes you loggy. I can't recall getting sick during a game, but I was one of the lucky ones. Paul Pryor, the same fellow who was locked in the bathroom in Houston, got food poisoning in Los Angeles. He had diarrhea and was vomiting all day.

The doctor told him to stay in his room, not to work that night, but Paul didn't want to miss the game. He had a streak going and told the doctor, "No, I'll be okay. I've got to work."

Ninety percent of the umpires are like that. If they can stand on their two feet, they'll work. Babe Pinelli's twenty-two years in the league without missing a game may have been the record, but other fellows had long streaks, too. Bill McKinley of the American League was another iron man. So was Ken Burkhardt, one of my old partners. Burkhardt was in the National League nineteen years and in all that time only missed two innings.

I remember one time Burkhardt had the plate in the first game of a doubleheader in Atlanta. It was so hot that day you'd have thought you were at the equator. Ideal weather for Sabu and his elephant. Burkhardt was felled by heat prostration in the seventh inning of the opener and, with great reluctance, agreed to go into our dressing room. We finished the game without him. The Atlanta team doctor told him to go back to the hotel, but Burkie refused and came back for the second game. He was proud of his streak. He didn't want to break it.

Paul Pryor had the same reaction. Food poisoning wasn't going to stop him. He was okay until the seventh inning. He was about to bend down for the next pitch and yelled to Johnny Roseboro, the Dodger catcher.

"Look out, John, I'm sick."

And Pryor upchucked right on the plate, in front of fifty thousand people. It was embarrassing. The ground crew had to come out with a bucket of sand.

Most of us, I'm convinced, must have cast-iron stomachs. The constant travel plays hell with your diet and your body. Nobody in professional sports travels as much as an umpire. The ballplayers are on the road for a week or two at a time, then they go home. We're always moving. Every third or fourth day we're in an airplane, and sometimes we have to fly all night to get to the next assignment on time.

We fly 100,000 miles a year and our bodies must constantly adjust. The travel is the most fatiguing part of the job. We're always resetting our watches because of the changing time zones. The toughest trips are from west to east, when you lose two or three hours. And there's the constant change in the weather. One day you're in Montreal and it's so cold you have to wear two pairs of long underwear and the next day you're working in Atlanta or San Diego in ninety- or hundred-degree heat.

Umpires are absolute experts on travel. If you want to know what the schedule is, say, on a Sunday night from Pittsburgh to Montreal or Pittsburgh to St. Louis, we not only know the arrival and departure times but we know the kind of equipment, if it's a DC-8 or 747, and sometimes even what the pilot has for breakfast.

Fred Fleig, the secretary-treasurer of the National League who is also in charge of umpire recruitment, makes up our schedules. We get a new schedule every three or four weeks. It's top secret. The league office doesn't want anybody to know our next stop or where we stay. This prevents the lunatic fringe from harassing us with telephone calls. The general managers and other executives from the individual clubs don't know either, not until an hour or two before game time, and then they've got to come down to our dressing room to see what crew is in town.

The logistics can get complex, especially with so many night games. It's easier for the ball clubs to get from city to city because they fly a lot of charters. We never travel with a club. We always go commercial. Many times a club can take off and go to the next city at midnight or one or two o'clock in the morning. We can't do that. We get a short night's sleep, four or five hours, and are on our way at six or seven o'clock the next morning. It was easier years ago, before expansion, when we had only eight teams in each league and never went to the West Coast or into Canada. We never went west of St. Louis, or south of Cincinnati.

Usually all four of us travel as a team. The only time we break up is if we have an open date and one of us is lucky enough to be close to home. Then the lucky fellow jumps and sees his wife and children for twelve to eighteen hours. That's the biggest drawback of the job, that we're away so much. A lot of guys get homesick. They're always moaning, "I never get home. I never get home." But they know this is the way it's going to be when they start umpiring. The season runs six months, early April until October, not counting spring training.

In a typical season I'll get home maybe fifteen or twenty days. And I live in New Jersey, which means I can skip home from New York or Philadelphia. Some guys who don't live near any major-league cities only get home during the midseason break for the All-Star game.

We make all of our travel and hotel arrangements. One man handles the travel and buys all the plane tickets. Another man contacts the hotels and a third man oversees the equipment bags. The crew chief is the overseer. We travel first class all the way. We used to get special service, a few extras here and there. In years past we'd check into a hotel and the hotel manager would be there to greet us, or have dinner with us. Not any more. Sometimes we have to argue just to get our rooms.

We don't stay at the same hotel as the ballplayers. There's no actual rule that we must stay apart, but it's a good policy. We see enough of the players at the ball park and they see enough of us. And if you're in a different hotel you're not likely to run into an irate player who wants to resume an argument that began on the field. The only city where we might be together is in Cincinnati, and that's because it's a small town, with only two or three large hotels.

We always try to get into a town at least five or six hours before game time. There is no league rule, but that's the way we like to do it. Usually we come in the night before. And we never, never take the last possible flight. We always have at least one backup flight so that if there is mechanical trouble, or an electrical storm, or any kind of delay, we can still get to the ball park on time.

In twenty-five years of travel, the only time I ever missed a flight was when a game went into extra innings, or if there was a long rain delay. I'm still thankful about one extra-inning marathon between the Cardinals and Reds in St. Louis. It was on a Sunday, and I had an open date the next day before opening a series in New York. I had known about this day off weeks in advance and told my wife, Margie, what time I'd be coming in. Margie and the kids always knew where I was at any given moment. I always sent them a copy of my schedule and they'd Scotch-tape it to the door of the refrigerator.

Margie didn't drive, but usually her cousin Steve would take her to the airport to meet me. For some reason, she didn't go the airport that night. I don't recall why but she was home waiting for me, watching television, and heard about a plane crash in St. Louis. The plane ran off the runway. They said they were withholding the passenger list, but in those days they did give the flight number. Margie burst into tears. It was my flight.

When I got to Lambert Field, the St. Louis airport, I heard about the plane skidding off the runway and I hurried to call Margie. She was so happy. She expected the worst. I explained what had happened, that it was an extra-inning game, and that I had switched to a later flight. After that, I never complained when a game went into extra innings.

Only once did I come close to missing a game. I was going from New York to Los Angeles and, as usual, had a backup flight. This was when the jets first started to come in. I was flying TWA, on a maiden flight, a brand-new plane. It was a beautiful morning in New York. Everything was fine. But about an hour and a half into the flight the pilot came on the intercom and said, "Ladies and gentlemen, we have to land in Kansas City." Kansas City is the headquarters for TWA, and I suppose instead of landing in Chicago he thought it would be best if he brought the plane into his home base.

They took us into one of those big hangars and said the delay would be no longer than a half hour. Then it was an hour, and an hour and a half. I was worried. I knew it would be close, because there was no other flight I could catch. So I called Stan Landes, one of my partners, and told him where I was and what had happened. Stan was a very fine umpire, a wonderful partner. He was always with you 100 percent.

He alerted the airport in Los Angeles and arranged to have someone there waiting to meet me. We landed at a quarter to eight, fifteen minutes before game time. In those days we traveled with our equipment bag so I was able to change clothes in the car. Back at the ball park, Stan was stalling. He came out late, and then kept going over the ground rules with the opposing managers. After the third time, Walter Alston, the Dodger manager, said, "Stan, we heard you the first time." But Stanley said, "I know, Walter, but it's a big game and I want to be sure." I only missed a half inning.

In the course of traveling we run into all kinds of weather. I saw two big rains in my life and both were in Houston—a year apart, almost to the day. I'd always heard they do everything big in Texas, but had been skeptical until those two rainstorms. I never saw so much water. These were more than rains; they were floods.

The first one was on June 9, 1975. In Houston we stay at the Tower Hotel, out near the ball park. We can see the Astrodome from our window. It rained most of the day, but my partners and I didn't think much about it because you can't get rained out in Houston. The Astrodome, of course, has a roof, the first enclosed ball park in the world. When it first opened, Judge Roy Hofheinz, then the owner of the Astros and the man who built the Astrodome, always insisted it was the Eighth Wonder of the World.

My partners were Billy Williams, Lee Weyer, and Satch Davidson, and we left the hotel together. The rain was so heavy that the main streets were full of abandoned and stalled cars. But Weyer, who is a very good driver, took a lot of side streets, and we got to the park in good time.

Spec Richardson, who then was the Houston general manager, was waiting for us in the umpires' room and said he didn't know what to do because only eleven of his twenty-five players had made it to the park. We put in a call to Chub Feeney, the National League president, and he told us to hold off making a decision until the last minute, but that if it was at all possible we should play the game.

There was almost nobody in the park, except the ushers and concessions people, who always report to work three and four hours before game time. At seven o'clock, a half hour before the game was scheduled to begin, Hub Kittle, one of the Houston coaches, called the ticket office to see if any fans were arriving. He was advised that at that point only five tickets had been sold at the gate.

Doug Konieczny, who was scheduled to make the pitching start for the Astros, was among the Houston players unable to get to the ball park. Tom Griffin started the game in his place. Tony Kubek, the TV announcer, was there and said it was the first time he'd ever seen a game rained in. When the game began there were about one hundred people in the seats. At the finish the crowd was about three thousand. It amazed me that that many people were able to get to the park.

A year and one week later, on June 17, 1976, I was back

in Houston and this time the flood was worse. Now I know what prompted Noah to build his ark. It began raining at three o'clock in the afternoon. An hour later I looked out the hotel window and noticed that traffic was starting to back up. I put the radio on and the forecast was for more rain. They were also issuing warnings that driving was hazardous, and that people should stay indoors.

We had to get to the ball park. I called my partners, John McSherry and Art Williams. McSherry was in his room, but Art was out with friends and had left word he'd meet us at the ball park. McSherry and I left the Tower Hotel and started off to the Shamrock Hotel, which is close by, to pick up Paul Pryor, the other member of our crew.

By the time we had driven a hundred yards the water was already coming in through the doors. We picked up Pryor. He was drenched, but waiting. From the Shamrock it's about a mile, at the most a mile and a half, to the Astrodome. We got halfway there when the car went dead. I felt like I was the captain of a whaling ship caught in a torrential storm. I bellowed to my partners, "Okay, men, let's get out. We can't sit here."

The water was now up to the hood of the car. I'll never forget what happened when we got out. The instant the doors opened, the water whooshed into the car. You'd have thought we were in the middle of Niagara Falls. We took off our shoes and took our money out of our pants and held both shoes and money over our heads. We started for the Marriott Hotel, about two blocks away, but the water was so deep we didn't know if we were on the street or on the sidewalk or on a parkway. We gripped each other's hands and kept going. It was cold, really cold, but what frightened us most of all was the possibility that we'd step into an open sewer.

It was bedlam at the Marriott. The lobby was full of people and all the phones were busy. The hotel manager got us a phone. I called Tal Smith, who had succeeded Spec

Richardson as the Houston general manager, and told him where we were, and that the only way we could get to the ball park was by rowboat and no boats were available. Tal said I had to get there because as the crew chief it was up to me to call the game off. I said, "You call it off and use my name." But he was afraid that was against regulations, so I told him to contact Chub Feeney at the league office in San Francisco. And so Chub called it off—the first and only rain-out in the history of the Astrodome.

The paper the next day reported that three people had died in the storm. An eight-year-old girl was sucked into one of the sewers. On the way back to our hotel we took a little old lady out of a car and brought her back with us. She was just sitting there—so scared she wouldn't get out of her car—but we finally coaxed her out. If we hadn't gotten her out she might have drowned. McSherry got an infected foot as a result of walking in the water. He must have stepped on something. And Art Williams had to see a doctor about his eyes. They were inflamed. He, too, had some kind of an infection. None of us will ever forget the big rain in Houston.

There's got to be a certain camaraderie among the umpires. We live together six months of the year and we get to know each other like our own families. I've seen one guy ruin a crew. The league office should take four guys who have a good chance of getting along together, but in my twenty-five years in the league nobody from the office ever asked for my advice on crew assignments. A lot of trouble could have been avoided with just one or two phone calls.

For the most part I was lucky. Billy Williams and I worked together for twelve years. We hung out together, liked to do the same things and go to the same places. He was like a right arm to me. Most of the time the two senior men hang out together, and the two junior men do the same. Which is fine, but I always believed that all four of us should get together off the field once in a while—for breakfast or dinner or for a drink after the game.

I've been on crews where it seemed like the only time we saw each other was on the field, almost as if we were strangers. Guys would finish working a game, get dressed, and say, "Okay, see you tomorrow." And they wouldn't see each other again until the next night. I don't say we should be together all the time. That's not good either. But the men on the same crew should become friends, good friends.

I always watched over the younger umpires. Sometimes a new man has some questions, or wants to talk without the other guys knowing about it. So I'd take him to breakfast.

The stereotype image of an umpire is that of a loner, a man without friends. This isn't true. We may not have many friends, but the ones we have are good friends. In Los Angeles, I always stayed with Jack Pike, who has a restaurant and motel in Glendale. In Philadelphia, Al Franchi, who owns a trucking company, provides each crew with a car. I've got some good buddies in Pittsburgh: a fellow named Harry Miller, who went to Seton Hall, and Joe Petraglia, a foreman in a boilermaker works, who takes us to and from the ball park in his Cadillac limousine. Newman Bray, a used-car dealer in Covington, Kentucky, across the river from Cincinnati, gives us his personal car. A lot of people go out of their way for the umpires.

Sometimes we will spot people we know in the stands and they'll wave at us. Umpires never wave back, and there's a good reason for this. You never know who's sitting next to the person you know. A gambler could be in the next seat, and if we were to wave back somebody might think I'm signaling to the gambler. No umpire has ever been convicted of throwing a game, or helping throw a game. We're all very proud of that.

I had a special signal for my family, which I used only

when I had the plate on national television. I'd call home before the game and tell Margie and the kids that in the sixth or seventh inning I would tip my cap. They always got a kick out of that. Whenever possible, I always wanted my wife and children to know I was thinking about them, that they were the most important people in my life.

I would always try to pick up things for the kids, usually a little keepsake. Once I brought home a six-foot teddy bear. I bought it at an auction in San Francisco. I should have had it shipped home, but I thought it would be more fun if I brought it home myself.

I was working my way east and lugged this big teddy bear with me to each stop. In Chicago, at O'Hare Airport, a woman said to me, "Hey, mister, can't you leave your teddy bear at home?" Other people made similar wisecracks. In Cincinnati, the clerk insisted I had to buy a separate ticket for the teddy bear because it would take up a seat. I refused and kept the teddy bear on my lap. One man offered me fifty dollars for it. Finally I got home, to the Newark airport, and Margie and the kids were there to meet me. The teddy bear was white and black with big brown eyes, a really beautiful stuffed animal. The kids were small then, and what I remember most is that when they saw the teddy bear they all burst out crying, especially Patty Ellen. They thought it was a real bear.

That was my first and last experience hauling a stuffed animal from one coast to the other, but I've probably worn out more than a half-dozen suitcases. We travel heavy. In addition to our personal luggage, each of us has an eighty-pound equipment bag. Everything we use on the field is in that bag—mask, chest protector, shin guards, underwear, shoes, and uniforms. Baggage is a special problem and is handled by a freight company. The freight company picks up the equipment bags at the ball park and delivers them to the umpires' dressing room at the next ball park. The league pays for the shipping of all equipment. The umpires carry only their personal luggage.

Once in a great while these equipment bags go astray. It always has amazed me that our bags aren't lost more often. These freight companies must have a delivery record of 99.9 percent. They're like umpires: they don't miss very often. But when they do, it can be a lulu. Once my stuff wound up in Paris, France. It took a week for them to get it back to the States.

At one time or another all of us have had to work in makeshift uniforms because our equipment didn't arrive on time. It's happened in the World Series, in playoff and All-Star games. And it even happened the day, in 1962, when the Dodgers opened their new stadium in Chavez Ravine. Al Barlick worked the plate that day in borrowed gear. But it was an unusual situation, because the three other members of Barlick's crew all had their equipment. Walter O'Malley, the owner of the Dodgers, led a big search for Barlick's stuff. It was like a treasure hunt. An usher found it the next day in an eighth-floor broom closet.

The odds against becoming a major-league umpire are tremendous. They must be something like three hundred or four hundred to one; that is, for every three hundred to four hundred young men who enroll in an umpire school, only one is likely to make it to the big leagues. Even with expansion, there are only fifty-two major-league umpires, twenty-eight in the American League and twenty-four in the National.

This year, in 1979, there will be one spot open—at the most—and only because Nestor Chylak retired. I don't know Chylak too well because he's been in the American League, but I know he's been one of the great umpires of our time. And now that Nestor has retired, it may be another five or six years before there's another opening.

With the advent of television, the number of boys and young men interested in becoming umpires has increased tenfold. A boy will see us on TV and say, "Hey, Mom, I want to be an umpire." When that happens Mom or Dad should take the kid to the nearest psychiatric clinic and have his brains examined.

We get mail from boys asking how they can become major-league umpires. I always answer them and I don't discourage them. But I point out the odds are against them. They just aren't aware of the competition. I get the idea some of them think they could walk right into a big-league park and start calling balls and strikes.

If a young man, or woman, doesn't get into professional ball it would be worthwhile to go to one of the umpire schools, because he can always go back home and work high school or college games. There is a constant demand for umpires to work amateur and semipro games. There are several schools in Florida. Harry Wendelstedt, the National League umpire, runs what used to be the Al Somers School, and there is the Sports International Umpire Training School in St. Petersburg, Florida, and the Bill Kinnamon school, which has sessions in Florida and also in California. The tuition is about $500 for a four- or five-week course, and includes room and board. Students range in age from about eighteen to forty and it's perfectly okay if you wear glasses.

It was easier when I broke into professional baseball. In 1949, for example, there were fifty-nine minor leagues with a total of 464 teams and more than nine thousand players. If each minor league used a two-man system, and most of them did, this meant they had to have 464 umpires working in the minor leagues. The minors were a tremendous proving ground; where you got your experience and worked your way up. But the minors have diminished terribly. Today there are nineteen or twenty minor leagues, one-third of what it was thirty years ago, and the job opportunities for umpires have decreased accordingly.

What's happened to the minor leagues is another story —you can do an entire book on it—but it seems a shame more fans aren't aware of baseball's rich, grass-roots tradition. There was a time when almost every good-sized city or town had a professional team and its own set of heroes.

Roger Maris of the New York Yankees broke Babe Ruth's one-season home-run record in 1961 when he hit sixty-one homers. But the real American home-run champion, for one season, is Joe Bauman, who played for the Roswell, New Mexico, club in the old Class C Longhorn League. Bauman hit seventy-two homers in 1954. Joe Hauser was another minor-league homer champ and hit sixty-nine for the old Minneapolis Millers in 1933, a quarter of a century before Minneapolis got a major-league franchise.

In those days the minor leagues were filled with ball-players, some of them trying to climb the ladder to the major leagues, and almost as many others on their way down, hanging on. In between, there were a few players, and umpires, too, content to stay right where they were, happy to play out the string in places like Nashville or Valdosta or Waycross, Georgia.

Television changed the baseball map. At first, the fans in these small and middle-sized towns and cities could stay home on Saturday afternoons and watch major-league clubs in action. A few years later they could stay home on Sunday, too, and before you knew it they lost interest in their local team. In some ways these fans benefited, but they also paid a price. They could no longer go down to the drugstore and see a professional player in the flesh and say hello and maybe talk to him for five or ten minutes. Minor-league baseball was a personal, intimate sort of experience for these fans. Now they're lost in the fog of the Nielsen ratings.

I've never known a major-league umpire who didn't spend some time working in the minors. It's like being an apprentice. When fellows talk to me about going into umpiring, and they're persistent, I tell them, "Okay, if you're that serious give yourself five years and by then, if you're not in the big leagues, or on your way, get into something else."

That's what Nick Colosi did. Colosi, one of the best, is now in the National League and has an unusual story. Most fellows start umpiring when they're seventeen or eighteen—certainly by the time they're twenty. Colosi didn't start until he was thirty-five. He was an incurable baseball fan, and had been in the restaurant business. He managed the San Remo Café in Greenwich Village and later worked at the Copacabana, a Manhattan nightclub where he was in charge of the captains and waiters, a good-paying job.

But Nick wasn't happy. All of his life he had dreamed of getting into baseball and, in fact, had begun working some sandlot games in Queens, amateur games. In 1962, two weeks after his thirty-fifth birthday, he mentioned to his wife, Frances, that he'd like to enroll in the Al Somers School. He said, "Honey, I'll give myself five years, and if I don't make it by then, I'll quit."

They had saved a little money, and Nick's wife, bless her, said, "You're the breadwinner. We'll do the best we can."

Nick didn't make it on schedule. He worked seven years in the minors before the National League hired him. But by the fifth year he knew both the American and National leagues were interested in him, and so he stuck it out. And, it should be noted, when Nick enrolled in the Al Somers School he wasn't the oldest fellow in his class.

Bill Klem, before he became an umpire, had been a

bartender and bookmaker. Jocko Conlan was a florist. Al Barlick worked as a coal miner. Augie Donatelli was a tail gunner on a B-17 during World War II and spent several years in a prisoner-of-war camp. Bob Emslie was a trap-shooter and George Moriarty a songwriter. Chris Pelekoudas was a Chicago cab driver. Shag Crawford worked as a haberdasher, and Jerry Dale and John Paul Pryor taught school. John Kibler and Frank Dascoli were state troopers. Billy Williams was a steamfitter.

Jack Sheridan, a famous umpire of the previous generation, was an undertaker. Germany Schafer, a ballplayer of that day, used to lead his buddies to Sheridan's mortuary. Schafer would stop at a ventilator and, in funereal tones, would warn: "Your time has come, Jack Sheridan." In a game at Detroit, Schafer disagreed with a call and turned to Sheridan, who had the plate, and said it again: "Your time has come, Jack Sheridan." Sheridan unloaded him.

I mention this to illustrate that umpires come from all walks of life. Ed Sudol, who recently retired after a long career in the National League, was shoveling snow one wintry afternoon at his home in Passaic, New Jersey. When he had finished, Sudol went to the corner drugstore and bought a *Sporting News.* The first page he turned to was an advertisement for Bill McGowan's Umpire School, which was in Florida. A beautiful young lady in a bikini, standing against a palm tree, was pictured in the ad. "That's the school for me," Sudol decided.

Bob Engel, who has been the president of the Association of Major League Umpires—that's our union—was working as a bellhop in Bakersfield, California. The umpires in the California State League stopped at Engel's hotel. Engel noticed that the umps never got up until one or two o'clock in the afternoon. "The hours look pretty good," Engel said, and off to umpiring school he went.

Others got the call at an earlier age. Bill Haller would

take the bus into Chicago and go to Comiskey Park, home of the White Sox. While his buddies were trying to get autographs from the players, Haller would wait outside for the umpires to get to the park and carry their bags. The late Charlie Berry, a distinguished umpire, and not Ted Lyons or Luke Appling, was Bill Haller's hero.

We even have two second-generation big-league umpires—Paul Runge and Gerry Crawford, both of the National League. Paul's father, Ed, was an American League umpire for eighteen years. When I retired after the 1976 season, Gerry Crawford took my place. I couldn't have been more pleased. His dad, Shag Crawford, had been one of my partners. Shag has another son, Joe, who officiates in the National Basketball Association.

I suppose you can say that Paul Runge and Gerry Crawford were to the manner born, that they had a built-in advantage because their fathers were major-league umpires. But the evidence suggests otherwise. Paul Runge was in the minors for ten years. After his seventh year, he got the "word" from two different sources that the American League definitely wouldn't hire him, that they didn't want a father-son combination.

Paul always insisted this wasn't so much league policy as it was league "politics." I've heard Paul say more than once that Charlie Berry had a personality conflict with his father and vowed to keep him out of the American League. Paul passed this information on to his dad and said his father, who by this time had retired, was so angry he wanted to call the league office and raise hell. But Paul didn't want him to do that. Eventually Paul got into the National League.

It wasn't easy for Gerry Crawford either. Gerry spent seven years in the minors and might have come up a season or two sooner. He could have replaced his father, who retired before I did, but Gerry believes the league didn't want it to appear that it was replacing a father with his son. There have been dozens of fathers and sons who have made the major leagues as players but, so far as I know, the Runges and Crawfords are the first to make it as umpires.

It's inevitable, of course, that the sons are compared with the fathers. Sometimes players and managers will use it as a weapon against the son. It can be a burden. Jim Marshall, when he was managing the Cubs, told Paul Runge, "You'll never be as good an umpire as your dad," after Paul had made a call that went against the Cubs.

A few other managers did the same, hoping to upset Paul. Gene Mauch, who is now managing the Minnesota Twins, told him, "Your dad wouldn't have called it that way. You'll never be the umpire he was. And you won't be here next year."

Naturally, these kinds of remarks were upsetting to Paul, but almost all managers are tough on new umpires. Paul came through fine, and as time went on and new players came into the league the comparisons diminished. I'm sure at least half the players in the National League today don't even know his father was a major-league umpire. Players aren't like fans. They don't know much about baseball history.

Umpires have often played Cupid. Ed Vargo met his wife through Al Barlick, who was then his crew chief. Vargo has been happily married ever since. Terry Tata, another National League umpire, was umpiring on the sandlots in Waterbury, Connecticut, his hometown. A mutual friend introduced him to Augie Guglielmo, who had worked in the National League and was now retired. Guglielmo gave Tata some tips on umpiring, and Tata liked him so much he invited him to his house for dinner. Guglielmo fell in love with Terry's mother and is now Terry's stepfather.

I don't know if there have been any umpire brother combinations in the major leagues, but Bill Haller's brother Tom was a major-league catcher, a very good one. Late in his career Tom was traded from San Francisco to Detroit, into the American League. By this time, brother Bill was an established American League umpire.

One year, when the Tigers were in the pennant race, Earl Weaver, the Baltimore manager, objected to Bill working Tiger games, on the ground that Bill was likely to give the edge to his brother. It was a stupid and arrogant assumption. If I had been the league president I would have fined Weaver for making such an accusation. If the pitch is on the black, I'd call my mother out on strikes. But Joe Cronin, then the American League president, not only listened to Weaver, but agreed with him and for the rest of that season Bill's schedule was adjusted so he didn't have to work any Tiger games. It was a big mistake by Mr. Cronin.

It wasn't until 1974 that the umpire schools began accepting students with glasses. Eyesight has been a traditional target of abuse for umpires. How many times I have heard the old cliché "Ump, you need glasses," or "Where's your Seeing Eye dog?" But there always have been players who wore glasses and, in fact, the big-league population of bespectacled players has grown in recent years, particularly since the advent of aviator glasses, which are considered very stylish.

Ed Rommel, a one-time knuckleball pitcher for Connie Mack's old Philadelphia Athletics, was the first big-league umpire to wear glasses. To show how little difference it made, Rommel's glasses went unnoticed. Frank Umont wore specs in a Detroit–Kansas City game and the wire services sent out big stories about how Umont broke with tradition. Finally, Rommel spoke up and pointed out that he had worn glasses a week earlier. This was in 1956.

I'm a big man, so I never experienced any prejudice in regard to physical size, but many smaller umpires always have insisted they were prejudiced against because of their lack of height. To some extent I know this is true. Cal Hubbard, a fine umpire, was a bear of a man, and after he became the supervisor of umpires for the American League he publicly acknowledged that he preferred men who looked like football players. Hubbard himself had been an all-pro tackle with the Green Bay Packers.

Dutch Rennert, who is only five feet seven, says his size held him back. Rennert worked fifteen years in the minors, a long, long time, and believes he would have been up to the major leagues much sooner if he had been a six-footer. Bruce Froemming feels the same way. Froemming and Rennert are about the same size, though Froemming is huskier. Chuck Tanner, who now manages the Pittsburgh Pirates, once told Froemming, when they were both in the minors, that it would hasten his advancement if he wore elevator shoes.

Harry Wendelstedt, who is six feet two and about 225 pounds, admits that a big physique is considered among the qualifications. When Wendelstedt enrolled in one of the umpire schools, an instructor told him, "Kid, you're big and you're ugly. You've got a good chance of going all the way." It's also a matter of record that Lee Weyer, who is six feet six, had a quick rise through the minors. Cal Hubbard took one look at Weyer and told him he wanted him for the American League. But the National League signed Weyer first, when he was only twenty-four years old.

Only four umpires have been elected to the Hall of Fame, and all but Hubbard were on the small side, five-ten or under. The first enshrined were Bill Klem and Tommy Connelly, both of whom were about five-eight or five-nine. Jocko Conlan was elected a few years ago, and he's only five-seven. I don't think height means a thing. It's what you've got inside that counts. An umpire gets respect by the way he handles himself, not by the length of his pants.

Weight is another story. The league offices don't like overweight umpires. They think it's unsightly and also believe too much weight slows a man down. Sometimes I have to agree with them, but I was always amazed at how quick and agile Stan Landes was, and Landes's weight fluctuated between 270 and 295 pounds. One year Stan went on a diet and lost about a hundred pounds, but it didn't make him a better umpire and he eventually gained it all back. John McSherry has a weight problem, too, but he jokes about it and says it's good for an umpire to be heavy because it gives him thicker skin. But, in fact, Fred Fleig, the supervisor of umpires in the National League at the time, didn't hire McSherry until after McSherry lost fifty pounds.

Fred Fleig had been our supervisor for more than twenty-five years. He and Al Barlick were constantly scouting umpires. They kept a file on minor-league umpires, just like ball clubs have on players. If Fleig and Barlick saw a fellow who showed promise, they brought him up for spring training and had him work fifteen or twenty exhibition games. They did this for at least two years before they made a decision. They also liked to meet the man's wife, which is a good thing. The most important asset an umpire can have is a good wife. I know, because I couldn't have made it without Margie.

I am sure I'll be accused of being a male chauvinist pig, but I'm dead set against women umpires. Baseball is a man's game, not a ladies' game. It's nice to have the ladies as spectators. They dress up the place, but they don't belong on the field, not as players and certainly not as umpires.

Women's lib has been successful in crashing a lot of previously all-male preserves, but there hasn't been a female umpire at the major-league level. I suppose eventually there will be. Promotion-minded owners such as Bill Veeck in Chicago, Charlie Finley in Oakland, and Ted Turner in Atlanta can be expected to push for a so-called Lady in Blue. But when the lady gets in, it'll be as a gate attraction, not because she can do the job as well as a man.

Three women have taken a shot at professional umpiring. The first two "retired." Mrs. Bernice Gera, who was first, departed in tears. She quit after one seven-inning game. Christine Wren was next. She worked in the minors for three years. The last word on her is that she has taken a leave of absence. Number three is Pam Postema, who has been working in the Florida Gulf Coast League.

Mrs. Gera went to court, charging she was being discriminated against, and in this regard I'll say one thing in her favor. She showed good endurance. Her legal battle took six years. The New York State Court of Appeals agreed with her contention that physical requirements for baseball umpires were unjustified and discriminated against women. Mrs. Gera was on the small side—about five feet two inches and 130 pounds. She was a housewife from upstate New York and had never worked anything more than amateur and semipro games.

Here is the report from the 1973 Official Baseball Guide that tells of her brief professional career.

Mrs. Gera, who hadn't umpired a single game in the previous three years, made her debut in Organized Baseball on June 24, 1972, in the first game of a scheduled doubleheader between Geneva and Auburn in the New York-Pennsylvania League.

She worked the bases in the opener. Three of her calls led to disputes, one of which resulted in the ejection of Auburn manager Nolan Campbell. Campbell stormed out to protest and followed Mrs. Gera across the field after she had called an Auburn player safe at second base and then had quickly reversed her call.

Mrs. Gera gave Campbell the thumb and explained to him she had made a mistake in originally calling the player safe. "Why throw me out," Campbell asked, shouting, "because you made a mistake?"

Two subsequent calls by Mrs. Gera also prompted milder protests from the Geneva Rangers, the host team.

Immediately after the seven-inning game, Mrs. Gera walked to the Geneva clubhouse and told general manager Joseph McDonough, "I've just resigned from baseball. I'm sorry, Joe."

With that, Mrs. Gera, still clad in her blue umpire's uniform, strode to a car and was driven off by friends. Witnesses said she had tears in her eyes.

I don't want the ladies in the audience to think I'm against women's rights. Women are equal to men in many ways; in some ways they're better. At first I admired Mrs. Gera's stand. I thought she was very sincere when she started her crusade and was dedicated to being an umpire. But, when I think about it now, years later, I think she did it mostly for publicity. She wanted to be the first woman umpire.

Immediately after Mrs. Gera quit, the *Sporting News* had a big story about her and asked many of the major-league umpires for their comments. Here's what some of them had to say:

AUGIE DONATELLI. "That's the best thing that ever happened to umpiring. I know it looks very easy. The fans sit up there and second-guess the umpires and say, 'I can do that good.' They see daylight and they think they can call every play. It's not that easy. The only thing I'll give her credit for was chasing the manager. She unloaded him. That was good. But she should have stayed and worked the second game."

DOUG HARVEY. "I felt this is what would happen. I can't imagine any woman being able to take the guff. I've been umpiring since I was seventeen. I've been in every league you can think of, but working amateur and semipro games is nothing. I can umpire that stuff walking backward in a snowstorm. It's a cinch. The first time I went into pro ball, it was a new world and the higher you go the wilder it gets. She ought to see what it's like where they play for big money—where a two-inch pitch is enough to slit an umpire's throat."

HANK MORGENWECK. "I know some of the fellows who have worked with her and they said she wasn't good. But they went along with her, more or less, because she was a woman."

LARRY McCOY. "There is no way they can take the abuse the way a man can. A woman's feelings are different. You see it all the time. As soon as something goes wrong, a woman breaks out in tears. I hate to see it. It churns you up inside. When I broke into the Midwest League in 1966, there were ten new umpires. Only three finished the season. You have to be thick-skinned. My first year, the manager at Cedar Rapids was on me all the time. He used to tell me, 'You're not only bad, but you're consistently bad.' "

LARRY BARNETT. "There were plenty of times I felt like crying myself."

BILL DEEGAN. "A lot of guys quit after their first game, too."

BILLY WILLIAMS. "I thought, if anything, she would last a season. After her long fight and struggle—and then being given the opportunity—I thought she would stick it out. It sounds to me like she had planned it this way, to work one game and quit."

Christine Wren, the second woman umpire, lasted three full seasons. She's in her twenties, and was able to stand the gaff better than Mrs. Gera, who was in her forties when she had her one day in professional ball. Ms. Wren put in two years in the Northwest League and another year in the Midwest League. She took a leave of absence starting with the 1978 season. Bill Walters, president of the Midwest League, said she was a good umpire, better than average on balls and strikes, and hopes she'll come back.

She was getting the standard Class A wage—and apparently that's the main reason she quit. A lot of men quit for the same reason. They don't want to take the vow of poverty. The last anyone heard, Ms. Wren was living in Seattle and making about $17,000 a year driving a truck for a parcel service. That's even more than the scale for a beginning major-league umpire.

I saw an item about Ms. Postema last summer in the *Sporting News*. Pedro Gonzalez, the manager of the Bradenton (Florida) Braves, got into a hassle with her. He bumped into her and knocked her off-balance during the argument. George MacDonald, president of the Gulf Coast League, fined and suspended Gonzalez for three days for giving the lady "a bump."

Maybe someday there will be a lady umpire. Who knows? I'm not Merlin. I can't tell what's coming next. There might be a day when there will be a whole crew of female umpires.

But umpiring, even when you're good at it, is never a piece of cake. The schedule grinds you down and injuries are a professional hazard. We wear a lot of protective equipment, but even so you can get hurt. The risk is greatest when you're working the plate.

I've had pitches hit me flush on my face mask. A day or two later after one such incident, a tooth filling fell out. That's happened to me twice. And you get hit on the arms and the legs and on the top of your head. Even a medium-speed fastball is coming in at you at eighty-five miles an hour. I've seen balls shear the button off a baseball cap.

I've been hit by line drives more than a half-dozen times. In 1975 in spring training, a bat broke in half and hit me above the shin guard. I was bruised and sore for a couple of days, but I didn't think anything about it. Then, after the regular season started, I noticed I had developed a lump above the right knee. Finally, I had surgery. They removed the lump; it was similar to a blood clot. I was out for a month.

All in all, I was a lucky fellow. I only had two severe injuries—and by coincidence, Leo Durocher was there both times.

On the first, I got hit in the mouth by a ball thrown by Carl Furillo and I lost eight front teeth; the second time was when I broke my leg on that play at first base in Chicago. Both times I was working first base, an unlucky position for me.

The Furillo play happened in the mid-fifties, during the days when the Giants and the Dodgers had their great New York rivalry. Durocher was managing the Giants at the time. It seems ironic, but the two guys involved in the play were Furillo and Jackie Robinson, both of whom hated Durocher's guts.

Hank Thompson of the Giants hit a line shot down the right-field line, a sure double. Furillo got the ball off the wall on the first bounce. He had a wonderful arm, maybe the best arm of any outfielder I've ever seen. Thompson knew it, of course. After rounding first and starting for second, he changed his mind and scrambled back to first.

Furillo threw the ball to Robinson, who was playing first. I hurried to the outside of the bag so I could see the tag. The lights in the Polo Grounds were very low. I saw Robinson's hand go up to catch the ball but he didn't catch it. I did! Right in the mouth!

I lost eight teeth on that play. The next day the Dodgers sent flowers to my house in New Jersey. Later, during the season, Robinson apologized for missing the ball. I knew he had lost the ball in the lights, and I told him, "Forget it, Jackie, it was just one of those things."

I went along for the next fifteen years without suffering more than the usual bumps and bruises. I had a lot of close calls, a lot of collisions, but I always managed to get up and walk away. Until that time in Chicago, that is, when Al Oliver of the Pirates collided with Paul Popovich in that bang-bang play at first base. They had to carry me off the field and call for an ambulance.

My good friend Eddie Sudol suffered a broken collarbone in 1977, just before he retired. I don't know why it happened, because the chest protector covers the collarbone. Eddie's protector must have been loose. I'm not mentioning this to frighten anyone away from umpiring, but any veteran umpire is always aware of the possibility of being injured. It goes with the job.

An umpire also needs endurance. It's a long season. You work twenty to twenty-five spring training games and then you work a 162-game schedule. Sometimes you work as many as forty to fifty days without a day off. And the bulk of the schedule is in the summer. As I said, I've lost as much as thirteen to fourteen pounds in a single game. It's a great way to keep your figure.

In the old days you really couldn't beat the hours. They had nothing but day games and the umpires got to the ball park five or ten minutes before game time. They walked right on the field, put on their caps, and said, "Okay, let's play ball." But times have changed.

Eddie Sudol holds the record for working the longest games. It was coincidence, of course, but he had the plate in three consecutive games involving the New York Mets and they went twenty-three, twenty-four, and twenty-five innings—in that order.

The twenty-three-inning game was the second game of a doubleheader that lasted ten hours and thirty-three minutes in actual playing time. It was on June 21, 1964, in New York, the San Francisco Giants against the Mets, and it was Father's Day. Eddie got to Shea Stadium at eleven o'clock in the morning. The first game took three hours and ten minutes. Thirty minutes later the second game began and this game took seven hours and twenty-three minutes—and there were no rain delays. He didn't leave the ball park until two thirty the next morning.

was walking off the field one night in Milwaukee and a fan was hanging over the box-seat rail, near the dugout. It had been a tough game, extra innings between the old Milwaukee Braves and the Cincinnati Reds. I'm about to walk by this fan when he takes off his glasses and says, "Here, Gorman, you need these glasses more than I do."

I took the glasses and kept on walking.

A week or so later Warren Giles, then the president of the National League, called me long distance. He told me he got a pitiful plea from this fan in Milwaukee who had written him a letter asking if I would please return his glasses. The lenses were special and couldn't be duplicated. I sent them back to him in the next mail. A month later my crew and I were back in Milwaukee and my friend was there, wearing his glasses. We had another tough game. I walked off the field, right past my bespectacled friend, but this time he never said a word. Not a peep. That's what we call giving them an education.

Many of the fans you meet like to make jokes. We hear them all the time, but everybody thinks he's being original. Or they stare at you as if you were subhuman, or not human at all, some strange creature that earns his strange living in a strange way. They can't just say, "It's nice to meet you, Mr. Gorman," or "Mr. Williams," or "Mr. Weyer," or whatever. They've always got to say something about your eyesight. We check into a hotel, and they say, "Well, here come the blind men." Once I was signing the register in Dallas and the room clerk said, "How'd you find the hotel? Amazing!"

Some umpires get angry and start arguments, but eventually they settle down and take it as a part of their job, a part of their lives, an occupational hazard. Some of them develop their own ways of coping with the jesters. In the early days, when we rode the trains from city to city, I was sitting with three other umpires when the conductor came through to collect the tickets. He looked at us and said, "Well, here's the three blind mice. Ha! Ha! Ha!" Larry Goetz had the tickets and refused to surrender them. The conductor threatened to stop the train and throw us off. I told the conductor to come back later and not say anything, and maybe we'd be good boys and give him our tickets. That was just outside Chicago. At about Gary, Indiana, he returned, Mr. Somber, and even humbled. Larry handed him the tickets.

We get letters you wouldn't believe. Make your hair stand up. They're going to blow up my house, steal my wife and children, make off with everything I own, kill me. I'm a crook, blind, a shame to the profession. They're going to have Congress investigate. They're going to call the commissioner or the league president. All because I called a player safe or out. Larry Barnett made a controversial call in the 1975 World Series, the only proper call in that situation. He got so many threats the FBI had an agent living with his family for two months.

Most umpires have unlisted phones, but eventually your number gets out. How I don't know. They call. They shout threats and obscenities, at all hours of the night. In the last six years I worked, I changed my number eight times. Other umpires do the same. Still we get calls. Sometimes our families see the letters and hear the calls. You can imagine the effects on family life.

It isn't pleasant, either, when your children go to school and their schoolmates take up the argument. At Shea Stadium once, I called a Met player out on a close call at the plate. Yogi Berra was managing the Mets. He really got on me and I had to chase him. I live in New Jersey, across the border from New York, surrounded by millions of Met fans. My son Kevin went to school the next day and his friends took up the argument. He came home and told me, "Dad, you got me in trouble again." I had to explain I was sorry. But that's an umpire's life.

Umpires know all about the ancient and inherent right of booing the umpire and cheering for the home team. On the field, during the heat of the game, fine. Be my guest. Go ahead and cheer your heart out. We couldn't care less, but please don't carry the rage off the field.

Home or away, all the teams are the same to us. And I say this knowing that most fans are convinced that many officials are "homers" and therefore the home team always has the advantage. They couldn't be more wrong. Baseball umpires have no "home" team. The league office tries to arrange our schedule so we have just as many games in Milwaukee as in St. Louis or San Francisco or Atlanta.

In certain cities the fans are louder than in others. Sometimes they can give you a headache. Like in Philadelphia. The Philly fans are knowledgeable. They know their baseball. But they're always yelling. They've got the fever and are yelling before the game starts. As soon as we walk out to the plate the so-called jokes begin. "Look," somebody will yell, "there's Gorman. Look at the head on him." Somebody else will shout, "Hey, Tom, who's your undertaker?" Or, "Hey, Tom, follow the white line. It'll get you to first base."

I say let them yell. It's relaxing. They let off steam. They can't yell at the boss or the wife. So they take it out on us. But I hate to see a little kid yelling insults. He doesn't know what's going on. Why should he abuse us? Usually it's because his father is a leather-lung. Like father, like son, unfortunately. But as long as the fans don't get out of line, it's okay with me. It's their game. They're the ones who pay to get in, and when they stop paying we'll all have to start looking for new jobs.

But you do have to manage the fans on occasion—and sometimes the sportswriters, too. One night, a few years back, in a Northern League game at Duluth, Minnesota, Bruce Froemming chased everybody in the press box. Emptied it except for the field announcer.

The press box in Duluth is right above the playing field and is as much a part of the field as home plate. The rules in the instruction manual are clear. The umpires have jurisdiction. Froemming had warned the so-called gentlemen of the press the night before, but they remained abusive. Finally Froemming told them to get the hell out of there. He threatened to forfeit the game, against Duluth, unless they left. They went.

I'm sure Froemming was justified, but that's a drastic remedy. I've never had to go that far, but I've often been tempted to clear out some of the leather-lungs. But don't get the notion that we believe all fans are obnoxious. Not at all. Ninety-nine percent of them are wonderful.

We get a lot of requests for photographs and auto-graphs. I'm constantly amazed that so many people collect baseball memorabilia. They have regular clubs in many of the major cities for such collectors. I still get birthday and Christmas cards. When I broke my leg in Chicago, on that close play at first base, I got more than five hundred get-well cards. A nice old lady brought me a box of candy. Two restaurants in Chicago sent food. I even got three mass cards—from people who thought I'd died.

Once in a while an umpire even has the fans on his side. A couple of seasons ago John McSherry—he and I were partners for several years—was working the plate in Los Angeles, one of those crucial Dodger-Cincinnati games. In the first inning McSherry had to run Sparky Anderson, the Cincinnati manager. A minute later, by co-incidence, the Dodger message board lit up and an-nounced, "Happy Birthday to Plate Umpire John McSherry." The scoreboard messages are prearranged. It had nothing to do with McSherry unloading Sparky.

Vin Scully, the Dodger announcer, mentioned it on the air and said, "Well, that's where Sparky went. He went to get John McSherry a birthday card." And then the fans began singing "Happy Birthday."

Later that same week McSherry had to chase a real live pigeon out of Shea Stadium. John was working a Met-Cardinal game, an important game because both clubs were still in the race. The Cardinals were rallying in the sixth or seventh inning and McSherry, out of the corner of his eye, spotted this pigeon in front of the Met dugout. The pigeon was just wandering around and McSherry ignored him. A couple of pitches later the pigeon was halfway between the Met dugout and the plate.

McSherry didn't know what to do. He figured the pigeon had a broken wing or a broken leg, that he was unable to fly. But he realized he'd look pretty silly if he started chasing it. Couple of more pitches later the pigeon was gone. McSherry was smiling. End of problem. Just then Nick Colosi, who was working third, called time-out and yelled to McSherry, "Hey, John, there's a pigeon behind you."

The fans were beginning to laugh. McSherry gave the pigeon the thumb. "Get out of here!" he yelled. The pigeon held his ground, but cricked its neck and looked up at McSherry as if to say, "Hey, who's this crazy guy in the blue suit?"

By now twenty-five thousand people were laughing like hell. McSherry kicked dirt at the pigeon but the pigeon didn't even back up. This was a New York pigeon, chased by subway trains, by trucks; he'd been caught in rush-hour traffic, knew his way around. A little dirt didn't bother him.

In desperation, McSherry walked closer to the pigeon and took off his mask. That was the end. The pigeon could take no more. One look at McSherry's face and he flew away.

This was in early September, in 1975. Later, McSherry laughed about it and said: "I got the pigeon and Sparky Anderson in the same week, and I'll tell you this, Sparky left easier."

I had to contend with dogs and cats, a few garden snakes, and I've had to stop games because of a swarm of gnats. For some reason, gnats usually congregate at the pitcher's mound. Different ball parks seem to attract different animals. Ebbets Field in Brooklyn used to lead the league in dogs. Cats are big in Candlestick Park in San Francisco.

As you go from city to city there is also a noticeable difference in the general deportment of the fans. I've never made a study, but in some cities the fans are much more reserved and quiet than in others. Houston, Texas, is quiet. You can hear a pin drop in the Astrodome. The St. Louis fans are well mannered. There can be forty thousand people in Busch Memorial Stadium and sometimes you hardly know they're there.

San Diego surprised me. As a general rule, when major-league baseball is new to a city, the fans aren't noisy. But in San Diego the fans sitting behind the plate call every pitch. Maybe they're amateur umpires, or just frustrated umpires. They were always helping me. I'm sorry I never thanked them.

When the Dodgers moved to Los Angeles the people out there sat on their hands for the first five years. Then, suddenly they started cheering and booing. San Francisco was quiet, too, but not anymore. A pennant race always makes the fans more vocal. You don't hear much anymore about the Bleacher Bums in Chicago, but when the Cubs were hot and almost won a pennant, in 1969, they were in the park and in their seats yelling two hours before game time. They were wild for a pennant. They reminded me of the old Dodger fans in Brooklyn. Devoted, dedicated, and loud as hell.

I notice there's been a Broadway stage play written about life in the Wrigley Field bleachers titled *The Bleacher Bums*. The Bleacher Bums were terrific, not only for the Cubs but for baseball. They were most prominent in 1969 when the Cubs almost won the National League pennant. They added to the excitement. If there was a call against the Cubs, on a close play, you could hear the boos all the way downtown to the Wrigley Building.

Chicago always has been a favorite stop for the National League umpires because the Cubs play nothing but day games. Wrigley Field is still the only major-league park that doesn't have lights. When you had the Cubs at home, you had your evenings free and could enjoy a nice, leisurely dinner. I've always considered the Cub franchise one of the best in baseball. Smallest park in the league, play nothing but day games, televise every day, and still draw a million and a half.

[*178*]

Like fans everywhere, some of the Bleacher Bums carried gloves and tried to catch home runs. This was fine so long as the ball was in the seats. Wonderful—they're entitled to a souvenir. Our only objection was when they would lean over the wall and either catch the ball or deflect it. That's what we call spectator's interference.

A few years ago John Holland, then the general manager of the Cubs, helped us out by hanging a wire basket level with the top of the wall. Now the fans in the front row can't interfere. If the ball lands in the basket it's a home run. No question about it. This problem doesn't exist in the new stadiums because the seats are higher or farther away from the wall.

Wrigley Field is a beautiful park, the only ball park with ivy on the outfield walls. The late Philip K. Wrigley, who owned the Cubs for almost fifty years, used to advertise "Come to the park for a picnic lunch." You couldn't blame him. He had to advertise something. The Cubs have gone longer without a pennant than any other club, not counting the expansion teams.

But Mr. Wrigley's walls of ivy can be a problem. Sometimes the ball gets stuck in the ivy and, in that case, it's a ground-rule double. Other times an outfielder will back into the wall to make a catch, and the ball might graze through a few leaves before it hits his glove. That's an out.

Last year when the Cubs were in the pennant race there was a big dispute on a play involving the ivy. Davey Johnson of the Cubs was the batter and hit a ball to left field. Warren Cromartie of Montreal ran to the wall for the catch. Cromartie leaped, the ball hit his glove and popped out, but Cromartie recovered and caught it on its way down, about waist high.

My old friend Herman Franks, the Cub manager, yelled that after the ball popped out of Cromartie's glove it also hit some leaves so there was no catch. Umpire Andy Olsen disagreed. First, Olsen told Herman the ball didn't hit any leaves and even if it did it would have been a catch because there was no solid deflection. Every time I see a house covered with ivy I think of Wrigley Field and the Bleacher Bums. Bless 'em.

The toughest park in the league is Atlanta, because the fence at the Atlanta Stadium isn't solid—it's chicken wire —and sometimes it's not easy to tell, especially in twilight, if the ball bounced over the fence or cleared it on the fly. Ted Turner, the Atlanta owner, should spend a few bucks and put in a solid fence. It would help keep our blood pressure down.

Spectator's interference used to be two bases, but now it's up to the judgment of the umpire. I'm responsible for that. It was put in the rule book after I went around and around with Birdie Tebbetts, when Birdie managed the Cincinnati club. Cincinnati opens its season a day ahead of the other teams. It's a tradition. Opening day there is always a sellout.

This particular rhubarb occurred at old Crosley Field. The crowd was so big it spilled out onto the outfield. The opposing team had a runner on first base. The batter hit a shot down the third-base bag and it bounced on the line. The guy at first base went all the way around to score, and the fellow who hit the ball was almost at third base when a fan picked up the ball, just as the outfielder was reaching down for it. But when this happened the play was almost over.

Tebbetts screamed and wanted two bases on interference, similar to a ground-rule double. He wanted the runner who scored to return to third and the batter held up at second base. This would have been unfair to the other team. To a certain extent there was a rule on the books for interference, though it wasn't specifically for fan interference. And so my ruling became a rule.

There are times, of course, when fans do more than interfere with a ball hit down the line. They can also get obnoxious and very personal with their insults. Sometimes you'd like to go into the seats and grab a guy by his collar. But we don't do that.

But there have been a few umpires, over the years, who had difficulty restraining themselves. Among them was the late George Majerkurth, a very colorful umpire. I saw Majerkurth work when I was a kid, growing up in New York. It wasn't until later that I heard about his reputation as a fighter.

Majerkurth was a huge man who in his youth was devoted to football and prizefighting. He brought the technique of both of those sports into baseball and so far as I know was one of only two umpires who ever ducked a pop bottle flung by a disapproving fan, picked up the glassware, and threw it back into the stands, winging the original thrower in the shoulder.

Harry (Steamboat) Johnson also threw a few bottles back, but one day in Memphis a fan got even with him. Months before, Steamboat had come out with his biography, *Standing the Gaff,* and this fan threw his book at him. Hit him in the head, too.

Steamboat was a beloved figure in the Southern League. Majerkurth also inspired unusual warmth among the paying customers. Once they took up a collection in the stands and raised a purse to pay the Maje's fine after he had punched a fan.

Majerkurth was always getting into fights. Once, in the minor leagues, he invited a particularly disagreeable manager to meet him under the stands after the game. Majerkurth punched him out. The incident made national headlines. The next day Majerkurth didn't show up at the ball park. This puzzled his partner because it hadn't been Majerkurth who was wounded, and if the league president had meant to suspend George he would have sent along a substitute umpire.

Investigation disclosed that the league president had

sent Majerkurth a telegram that read: WIRE FULL REPORT ON FIGHT STOP WORK TODAY.

Obediently, the Maje had stopped work. But he never again had any faith in Western Union.

The most famous of Majerkurth's scraps occurred in 1940, late in the season, after the last out in a ten-inning game at Ebbets Field between the Dodgers and Cincinnati. The Dodgers lost 4–3 and a fan jumped down on the field, wrestled Majerkurth to the ground, and got in a few good punches. It was one of the few fights Majerkurth lost.

A photographer got a picture of the scuffle. It was embarrassing to the Maje because his assailant, though stocky, was about half his size. Later, during the arraignment, it was revealed that the assailant was a convict on parole after a petty larceny conviction. Majerkurth took a benevolent view and withdrew the complaint. "I'm the father of a boy myself," the Maje said.

There was an echo of that skirmish more than ten years later when Red Smith, the famous New York columnist, was having lunch with Brooklyn Judge Samuel Liebowitz. During lunch, they recalled the day Majerkurth was attacked by the fan.

"There's a sequel to that story," Judge Liebowitz revealed to Smith. "A couple of years later that same little fellow came up before me to be tried as a pickpocket. He was tried and convicted. All through the trial I kept looking at him, trying to remember where I could have seen him before. I knew his face, but I couldn't place him.

"After the verdict, I said to him, 'Don't we know each other? I'm sure I've seen you somewhere.'

"He was a cocky little guy and said he'd been around. He had a record as long as your arm. I tried a shot in the dark.

" 'Ebbets Field?' I said.

" 'That's right,' he said, 'Ebbets Field.'

" 'Why,' I said, 'you're the fellow who jumped on George Majerkurth.'

" 'I did indeed,' he said. He was mighty proud of it.

" 'Tell me,' I asked him, 'how did you come to lose your head that day? Were you really all that stirred up because the Dodgers lost the game?'

" 'I was pretty stirred up,' he said. 'I was mad enough to slug Majerkurth, all right. The Dodgers shoulda won easy. But just between you and me, Judge, I had a partner in the stands that day. We wuz doin' a little business.'

"The little bum," Liebowitz said, "was just creating a disturbance so his partner could pick a few pockets."

portswriters can be a pain, some of them. You would think sportswriters and umpires would identify with each other. We have a lot in common. Many of us are about the same age. The sportswriters see players come and go. The evolution in baseball is constant. There is always a new generation of players. More than that, our jobs are similar. We're there to see that the game is played according to the rules, and the sportswriters are there to give an unbiased account of what goes on. But many times the players and managers are angry with objective reporting. They want the edge there, too, just like they want the edge in balls and strikes. They only want their side of the argument to get in the paper. Very few of them are interested in the whole truth and nothing but the truth.

Umpires are more independent. We have no affiliation, no identification, no obligation to any single club. Sportswriters are assigned to the team in their city. They travel with this team and become friendly with the manager and the players. They become cheerleaders for their club, sometimes super-fans. They get angry if we make a decision that goes against their club. Some sportswriters are so naïve they think the players love them, particularly if they're always writing nice stories about them, telling everybody how good they are. Sportswriters are foolish if they believe the players are their buddies. Across the board, the players have as much love for sportswriters as they do for umpires—and that's not much.

Yet the sportswriters rarely print our side of the story. If we eject a player or manager, the writers hurry to the clubhouse to interview him and they believe whatever the players and managers tell them. The printed version is seldom accurate. The umpires are also available for comment, but the writers are in a hurry and don't have time to talk to us. They've got deadlines. But more than that, they don't want to give a balanced account because then their players and managers will be angry with them. So our side is ignored.

I'll give you an example. In the 1977 World Series, Nestor Chylak supposedly made a bad call on a play at the plate. Maybe it was a bad call. I don't know. If it was, I'll say this: for every bad call Chylak made, he made 499 good ones. He was one of the great umpires.

The next day, Wick Temple, the general sports editor of the Associated Press, wrote a story that went all over the country saying that Chylak was out of position when he made the call, and suggested that instead of using umpires, baseball should use cameras and go by the results of so-called instant replay. This Associated Press story probably ran in five hundred or so papers and, of course, Wick Temple set himself up as the big expert.

A friend of mine, a knowledgeable baseball reporter, called Temple and asked him how he could be such an expert, so sure of himself, and asked him how many ball games he had covered. Turned out that Temple had almost no experience covering baseball. Reluctantly, Temple admitted this. So this veteran reporter said to him, "Don't you know that Nestor Chylak is probably the most respected umpire in the American League?" No, Temple didn't know that. Didn't he know that the instant replays almost always show that the umpires are right? No, he didn't know that either. Then Temple said, "Well, I probably could have written this story from the umpires' side as well as from this side." He didn't do that because he "also knows how the average person feels, the guy who is watching the game on television." And this is a reporter who is the national sports editor of the Associated Press, which prides itself on being objective.

Another thing is that, with most writers, the only time we ever see them is on a controversial play. They come charging into our locker room. Most of the time we don't know who they are and they seldom pay us the courtesy of identifying themselves.

One night in Atlanta, we had a ball that either bounced or went over the fence on the fly, a tough call because of that damn chicken-wire fence they have there. Harry Wendelstedt called the play and we had a helluva rhubarb. And this guy comes in, hollering and screaming at us, wanting to know how the hell we could make that call. I almost threw him through the door. Turns out this guy, this "homer," is Furman Bisher, an Atlanta columnist, and he blisters us in the paper the next day. Now if he had told us who he was, we would have been glad to answer his questions, to let him have an interview. Later the league office gave us some heat because we weren't courteous to Mr. Bisher, the big sportswriter.

A guy I did throw out was Joe Falls of Detroit, also a columnist. This was many years ago, in spring training, when Rocky Colavito was with the Tigers. Colavito started an argument with Franny Walsh. Bob Scheffing, the Tiger manager, came out to help Colavito. Franny chased Scheffing.

The game ended and in came Joe Falls, the big Tiger booster. Rah-rah guy. Didn't knock on the door. He said to Walsh, "Did you throw Bob Scheffing out?"

"I sure did," Walsh said.

"Then why didn't he leave? He managed the rest of the game from the dugout."

This was Franny's first year in the big leagues. The whole scene made me angry, not the questions but the way they were asked, the fact that he came barging in and didn't even tell us who he was. I walked over, picked him up, and carried him to our door, and out.

I met Falls years later. Not a bad guy, and they tell me he's a good writer. I understand he's also since learned a few things about courtesy.

In general, we have no problem with the so-called media. Some of them give us an honest count and even say hello. We go on radio shows and give interviews, though we're asked only after we've been involved in a controversial play. I've never heard of an announcer who told an umpire, "You had a helluva day today. Eight bang-bangers and you got 'em all right. Will you come on the air and tell the secret of your success?" They don't do that. It's after you've been fried in oil by the fans and the press, that's when they say, "Hey, Tom, c'mon on, you get a free clock radio."

We all have our favorites, and one of the guys I like is Jack Brickhouse, a television guy out of Chicago who travels with the Cubs. I understand he fought with Durocher and, of course, that doesn't make Brickhouse bad. Who in the hell didn't fight with Durocher? Leo didn't just give umpires a hard time. He fought with the press and the radio and TV guys, too.

Mr. Brickhouse is the announcer who got baseball into the space age. His station, WGN-TV, is in the record book: "First live intercontinental telecast of a game, or portion of game, July 23, 1962."

It was decided that the Europeans, on this historic day, should see part of a baseball game—the Chicago Cubs vs. Philadelphia Phillies at Wrigley Field. They also showed other things of interest such as the Golden Gate Bridge in San Francisco, Cape Canaveral, and Niagara Falls. The Cubs and the Phillies were to be on for only ninety seconds.

Mr. Brickhouse was worried and before the game sought out the late Tony Venzon, a very good umpire, a good friend. Tony had the plate that day. Brickhouse was afraid that his ninety seconds could come and go without anything happening in the game. What if the batter took a couple of pitches in a row? If that happened, the people in Europe could get the wrong idea. They would think that baseball is a dull game. No action.

"Don't worry, Jack, I'll take care of it," Tony told him.

Brickhouse figured that Venzon was being optimistic, merely trying to calm him down and assure him everything would be okay. Tony said, "I'll keep looking up at the booth. Give me a signal when you're about to go on."

"I'll do better than that," Brickhouse said. "I'll have it announced over the loudspeaker system."

In the sixth inning, Phillies at bat, Cal Koonce pitching, the ball game went on intercontinental television. Tony Taylor of the Phillies was batting and hit the first pitch, a drive to right that was caught by George Altman. Johnny Callison was the next batter. He, too, swung at the first pitch and singled to right.

That ended the ninety-second baseball telecast. Brickhouse was delighted. He hurried to the umpires' room and told Venzon, "IIey, Tony, we sure were lucky, both of those guys swung at the first pitch."

"Lucky, hell," Venzon says. "That was my doing. I told them, 'Fellows, you better swing at anything this guy throws, because if it's within three feet of the plate it's going to be a strike. We're on international TV, and I don't want those Europeans to think baseball is a dull game.' "

y wife was the greatest
individual in the world. You talk about two people crazy
about each other, and crazy about baseball, that was us.
She was a very warm person, an angel. If she liked you,
you had a friend for life.

She went through a lot, but never complained. The
minor leagues were tough. I made $160 a month and the
first couple of years all we could do was eat sandwiches.
We couldn't afford anything else. It seemed like every
week I was spending twenty, thirty dollars, just to get my
car fixed.

We didn't have enough money to support two homes.
On what I was making, I couldn't even support myself.

When you're an umpire in the minor leagues, it's like being a priest. You take the vow of poverty. Without her I couldn't have made it, and I know a lot of umpires say the same thing about their wives.

I used to lie in bed at night and say to myself, "What the hell am I doing here? Am I doing the right thing? I'm umpiring and I've got all the players yelling, and the leather-lungs are hollering from the stands. Is it worth it?"

Margie never complained about my being away from home. She didn't drive, but whenever possible she would take the bus and meet me on weekends. Even when I was in the Three Eye League, which is in the Midwest, she'd take that long bus ride so we could have a few hours together.

She worked at IBM as a secretary, and wouldn't get to Davenport, Iowa, or Decatur, Illinois, until two or three o'clock Saturday morning. We'd have the rest of that day together. There would be a doubleheader on Sunday and she would have to get back on the bus at noon and ride all night to be on time for work on Monday morning.

People never realized what she went through. But we were young and in love and happy, and weren't aware of all the sacrifices.

Margie loved to go to the games. She and the kids would go to spring training with me. If the World Series was in New York she'd go with me. Bobby Thomson was her favorite and the Giants were her favorite team. She was very upset when Horace Stoneham moved the Giants to California.

Every year, before the regular season opened, the Giants would go up to West Point for an exhibition game. It was enjoyable, a two-day excursion, and Margie and the kids would go with me. This was at the time when Leo Durocher was managing the Giants and when he was married to Laraine Day. Margie liked Durocher. She thought he was a good manager.

Before the game one time, we were having lunch and Laraine and Leo came over to our table. Leo said, "Tom, why don't we give the boys a little show today. You chase me. About the fourth inning."

"Sure. Be my guest," I said.

So, in the fourth inning I chased him. We put on quite a show. The cadets went bananas.

After the game Leo was very gracious and invited me and my family to have dinner at the Bear Mountain Inn. There was a special room set aside for the ball team. Toward the end of dinner, Leo came by and said hello to Margie and her aunt, Frances, who was with us. Frances had never met Leo before and was very impressed. When he meets women, Durocher puts on the charm.

"Frances, are you Margie's sister?" he asked. "You look so young." He gave her his full line of bullshit.

Then I introduced him to Tommy, my oldest son. Tommy was a big kid and Leo says, "Did you eat all that steak?"

Tommy says, "No, I only ate half of it. My father finished it."

I could have knocked the kid off his chair for suggesting I was taking food out of his mouth.

Two weeks later we're in the Polo Grounds. There was a bang-bang play at first base and out comes Leo, hollering as usual. I took it for a few minutes and I said, "Okay, Leo, you've had your say. I don't want to hear any more."

He took five or six steps and said, "Hey, Gorman, you still eating the kid's steak?"

I have four wonderful children, but it took me and Margie a while to get started on a family. We were married eight years before we had our first child. Finally, we both went to the doctor to get examined. Everything was fine with her, and so she said, "Why don't you get examined?" Here I am, a big strong guy, but I went to the doctor and he told me everything was fine.

When he walked me out of his office, into the waiting room, there were a couple of girls sitting there and he told them, "You better stay away from this guy. He's alive. I hope he's got his fly buttoned."

Margie was sitting there, too. She got a big kick out of that.

She got pregnant when we were in Cuba, and when we got home we had Tommy. Then Patty Ellen came along and Brian and Kevin. In a little less than six years we had four children. Once we got going we were hard to stop.

Tommy went to Marquette. He's now in the arts, a painter. I had a play in the 1974 World Series between Oakland and the Dodgers. Sal Bando was on second base and tried to score on a hit to right field. Joe Ferguson, who has a great arm, was playing right field for the Dodgers and threw him out. The play wasn't even close. Bando couldn't believe it. There was a photograph of the play in the paper and Tommy made a painting from that picture. I've got it hanging in the den.

Patty Ellen, the second oldest, was a World Series baby. I wasn't home for the others, but I was home for her. Now the umpires, as a result of our union, can go home when their wives are having babies. It used to be that they considered that just another day. Patty Ellen was valedictorian at Fairleigh-Dickinson. I remember going to the hospital when Margie had Patty Ellen. Margie liked Manhattans. It was against hospital regulations, but I'd sneak them to her in a paper cup.

Kevin was born in late March, when I was in spring training. Margie waited so long before going to the hospital she almost had him in the car. He's now at Monmouth College and looks like a good ballplayer. A good-hitting outfielder.

Brian, the youngest, is a sophomore at the University of Delaware. He's a very good soccer player and good at fixing things. I can't put a nail in the wall, but Brian can build cabinets. You name it, he can do it. All of the kids, of course, were accustomed to getting the raspberries at times from kids in school. Brian may have had it toughest. He went to school with a lot of Met fans. I know he had a few fights in the schoolyard, but he knew how to handle himself. One day one of his classmates said to him, "How do you feel when your father misses a play?" He told this kid, "I never have to worry about that because my father never misses a play."

It was a great shock when I lost Margie. If I was down, she always bucked me up. Sometimes if you have a tough game you bring it home with you. She was wonderful in every way, not just with me, but with everybody. I never saw a better mother, or a better friend. I never knew anybody who was nicer with people than Margie.

When we were in Cuba, there was a fellow there named Andre. We bought meat at his butcher store. Andre and his people were careless, very sloppy the way they threw the meat around. After we got to know Andre, Margie helped him clean the place up. She showed him how to put flowers around, make the place look more attractive and the meat more appetizing.

Andre couldn't get over it. He was so pleased. Christmas came around and Margie sent Andre a gift. It was the first gift he ever got. He didn't understand, and Margie told him, "Well, you're our friend and we exchange gifts with our friends." I'll be a sonofagun, Andre starts crying and goes out and buys gifts for me and Margie and for Margie's aunt, who was staying with us. I've often wondered what happened to Andre. I wouldn't be surprised if he stood up against Castro and Castro had him knocked off. A lot of people we knew down there fought for the country and were killed.

Margie died in 1968, the same year I worked the World Series between St. Louis and Detroit. She didn't know she was going to die. I lost her so soon, so quickly. She had never been sick a day in her life, never been in a hospital except when she was giving birth. She had a kidney infection, and within two weeks she was dead. She went into a coma two days before she died. She was only forty-six years old.

You remember little things, sometimes, about people you've loved. Once I was in Washington and got to see President Kennedy, whom both Margie and I admired a lot. I was speaking at a luncheon, downstairs under the Rotunda. I didn't know it, but President Kennedy slipped in through a side door and was in the audience.

After the luncheon, Dave Powers took me up to the Oval Office to meet the President. And to show you the kind of man he was, President Kennedy got up from behind his desk and walked over to meet me. He said, "Tom, I never enjoyed anything so much in my life. I laughed so much I almost wet my pants."

He also said, "You know how to handle people and you like people," and I agreed. I do like people. Then he asked what he could do for me, and I told him that Margie was at the hotel and would enjoy meeting him. He told me to bring her over the next morning.

Now, if you went home and told your wife that tomorrow morning she was going to meet the President of the United States there would be three things she would do. First, she would say she didn't believe you. And then, after convincing her, she would say, "Well, I've got to go to the hairdresser's." And the next thing she would have to do is buy a new dress.

It became one of the great days of our life together. Jackie Kennedy took her on a tour of the White House, and then we were escorted into the President's office. The President was very gracious, just wonderful. He asked Margie if there was anything he could do for her.

She looked at him and laughed a little, in shyness, I

suppose. "Yes, Mr. President, there is something." I was startled. What was she going to say. Then she asked, "Could I sit in your rocking chair?"

He said, "Be my guest."

And she sat in the chair awhile, rocking and smiling.

I was home for about a week before Margie died. I buried her on a Friday afternoon and at one o'clock the next afternoon the phone rang. Warren Giles, who was then the National League president, was calling and asked me to come back to work. He wanted me umpiring the next day. I blew my cork and almost quit. I said, "For God's sake, Warren, I've got four kids here. I've got to stay here a few more days and make arrangements. I'll come back to work when I'm ready, if I do come back."

Later, Warren told me he was thinking of my welfare, that he was trying to get me back to work and get my mind occupied. But that's the way it was in those days. If someone died, they gave you a day off and expected you back the next day. Now they give you three or four days.

At first I hired baby-sitters to take care of the kids. After a while, two good friends of ours, Charlie Gadek and his wife, Terry, moved into our house and stayed with us for two years. They were the biggest help I ever had.

It was rough without Margie, but the kids pitched in, especially Patty Ellen. She helped run things. I could never praise Patty Ellen enough. But it's never been the same without Margie. I'm always saddened when I hear about a man losing his wife, or if a friend of mine gets divorced. I don't know how they do it, how they survive.

Margie didn't only take care of the kids and the house. She was a great sports fan. She was proud of me in every way. I'll never forget the time she got into a dispute with a sportswriter named Russo who covered baseball for the *Bergen Record* in New Jersey. One year we got new uniforms, lighter ones, more comfortable than we'd had. Russo liked to take cheap shots at the umpires and he wrote that it didn't make any difference what uniform I wore, I still looked like an unmade bed.

I thought it was funny, but she didn't. "He's got a lot of nerve," she said. "You're a good dresser. You pay a lot of money for your clothes. I'm going to call him."

She called him at home. She called him at his paper. She left notes for him. She wouldn't give up. Finally Russo called back, to shut her up, I suppose. I don't know what she told him, but it must have been something fierce. At least it was effective. He said in his column the next day that he hadn't meant it the way he'd said it. That was shortly before Margie died. He sent flowers and attended the funeral. "I never met your wife," he told me, "but I respect her, the way she stood up for you."

If he'd known her as well as I did, he wouldn't have been surprised.

aseball has been good to me and I have no complaints. But I must admit that the best thing the umpires did was to organize into a union. It was done in secrecy in 1963. The National League umpires organized first. We invited the American League umpires to come in but they weren't interested. Why, I don't know. We guessed at the time that maybe Joe Cronin, who was then the American League president, threatened them. Five years later, after much grief, they woke up and joined our union and we changed our name to the Association of Major League Umpires.

Augie Donatelli deserves a lot of the credit. The union was Augie's idea and he did most of the hard work. Many umpires never properly thanked Augie, but if it wasn't for him they wouldn't be getting the salaries and benefits they have today. Most of us were satisfied with the little we got. Augie was always telling us we were wrong. He would say, "They kick us around like a rubber ball because they know they can get away with it." A lot of people resented Augie because of this, but he was right. We got a lot more respect, and more money, after we organized.

Augie and Shag Crawford, Al Barlick, Stan Landes, Jocko Conlan, Mel Steiner, and myself were in on it from the beginning. We had our first meeting in Chicago and Jocko found a lawyer for us, Jack Reynolds, a big, friendly guy who was an experienced labor negotiator.

I was in favor of organizing, but I didn't want to do it without mentioning it to Mr. Giles, the National League president. I said, "Let's take our complaints to Mr. Giles first. He's our boss. We should tell him what we're planning to do and maybe he'll help us."

Some of the other umpires, fellows who weren't at the meeting, agreed with me, but I was voted down. Maybe I was naïve. I still think we could have given Mr. Giles this courtesy. I never regarded him as our enemy.

When we announced we had organized, most of the people in the league office laughed at us. They didn't think we were serious. But we were. There were two owners who did go to bat for us, though, Walter O'Malley of Los Angeles and John Galbreath of Pittsburgh. They were surprised when they discovered our salaries were so small.

Reynolds negotiated our 1964 contract and we were on our way. When he took over, our starting salary was about $7,500 and the average was about $13,000. Our pension was pitifully small, $150 a year for every year of service: a fellow who had been in the league twenty years got $3,000 a year. Babe Pinelli, for example, put twenty-two years in and retired with a pension of $187 a month. Besides, part of our salary went into the pension fund so, in effect, we paid for our pension along the way. We also contributed half the costs for what even in those days was an inadequate medical and hospital program.

In the next ten years we made a lot of gains. By the time Reynolds left us, there were considerable pension and hospitalization improvements, death benefits, including benefits for widows, and the starting salary was up to $12,500. We also got a better money deal for working the playoffs and the World Series. In addition, we now have tenure after six years, that is, once an umpire is in the league for six years he can't be dismissed without the league showing good cause.

One of the benefits of organizing was that it brought all the umpires closer together and gave us a chance to know one another. The fans probably don't realize this, but in the old days the umpires never saw each other after spring training, and even in spring training we didn't always meet. Some of us worked in Florida and some in Arizona. We could go for a full season and the only umpires we ever talked to were our partners. I was in the league five years before I came face to face with Babe Pinelli. It was six years before I met Dusty Boggess.

John Cifelli, an attorney from Chicago Heights, Illinois, replaced Reynolds. Cifelli did a good job for us, too, but was succeeded in the spring of 1978 by Richie Phillips. I don't know much about Phillips, except that he's a young and aggressive Philadelphia lawyer who also represents the officials in the National Basketball Association. Cifelli got the starting wage up to $17,500; by this time some of the senior umpires were earning as much as $40,000. I was in the $40,000 bracket when I retired, pretty good considering I made $5,000 my first year in the league.

We couldn't have made all these gains if we hadn't stood together. Even with a union and with the help of professional negotiators, it wasn't easy. There were a lot of heartaches. Reynolds led us on a one-day strike in 1971. We struck the first game of the playoffs, the first strike by the umpires in baseball history. We didn't want to go on strike and hurt the good name of baseball, but we were forced into it. They were taking good care of us at the time but not good enough. We were fighting for a contract. Last year, in 1978, the umpires had another one-day strike but were immediately called back to work by a Philadelphia federal judge. There was a difference in the two strikes. The second one wasn't quite legal, because the umpires walked out when they were in the second year of a five-year contract.

It wasn't until after the 1968 season that the American League umpires joined our association. When they did, all hell broke loose and Joe Cronin, the league president, fired two fine umpires, Bill Valentine and Al Salerno. Cronin insisted they were incompetent and managed to fool the courts, but he didn't fool the umpires or anyone else wise to the inner workings of baseball. It was a sad chapter in the history of the grand old game. Salerno and Valentine got the ax for only one reason—because they had taken the initiative in organizing the American League umpires.

Our association brought charges against Cronin and the American League with the National Labor Relations Board. Salerno and Valentine also filed individual suits, each of them asking for about $2 million in damages. The thing dragged on and on and, in the end, we were the losers. The NLRB dismissed the charges for "insufficient evidence."

But for a while, before the case was heard and when it looked like we had a chance of winning, the American League agreed to reinstate Salerno and Valentine providing they dropped all charges and agreed to return to the minor leagues for a two-month "review," sort of a "tryout." This would make it appear they had improved as umpires and was a face-saving gesture for Cronin and the league.

Automatic reinstatement would follow. In addition, Salerno and Valentine would be given $10,000 each, as a salary settlement for the 1969 season, which they missed. They would also receive pension benefits retroactive to the date of their dismissal and would return to the American League at a salary of $20,000 a year, the new scale for umpires in their classification. This was $8,000 more than they were making when they were fired. It was to be a secret arrangement. The league refused to put it in writing.

Valentine was agreeable but Salerno refused and the deal was off because the league insisted there would be no settlement unless all charges were dropped. Valentine was very upset and went to Salerno's home in Utica, New York, and pleaded with him to go along with the arrangement. Later, the league upped the ante and promised to give them each $20,000 as compensation for the 1969 season. Again Salerno refused. Valentine, in his testimony, said he told Salerno he would give him, with no strings attached, half of his $20,000 settlement but Salerno said this sum still wouldn't cover his legal fees.

We found out who our friends were during the hearings. Only three American League managers came to the trial and testified in behalf of Salerno and Valentine. They were Eddie Stanky of the Chicago White Sox, Dick Williams who then had the Boston Red Sox, and Alvin Dark of the Cleveland Indians. They surprised us. All of them were pretty tough on umpires, especially Stanky.

Stanky, when he took the stand, said major-league umpires were among the most underpaid group of professionals in the country and insisted, "When umpires come to the majors they are competent." Asked to define competence, Stanky replied: "Knowing the rules and calling them the same way in every city, playing no favorites." Stanky, Williams, and Dark also said if they had to grade Salerno and Valentine in relation to other umpires, they would put them in the top half.

Originally, our association, by unanimous declaration,

agreed to boycott the 1969 spring training exhibition season if Salerno and Valentine hadn't been reinstated. But this promise was lost in the shuffle. Later, when Salerno balked and refused to drop his suit, some of the umpires insisted we no longer had any obligation.

Salerno is still bitter. From what I hear he's writing a book knocking baseball. He was recently quoted as saying, "If every baseball stadium in the country blew up tomorrow, I'd be happy." It's a shame he feels this way.

As for Valentine, he doesn't seem to have any ill feelings. If he does, he doesn't say so. He is now back in baseball and is the vice-president and general manager of the Little Rock, Arkansas, Travelers of the Texas League, a St. Louis Cardinal farm team. A few years ago he was honored by the *Sporting News* as the Minor League Executive of the Year.

Ron Luciano, a bright guy, is now the president of the association. He was graduated magna cum laude from the University of Syracuse and can match his intellect with anybody. After the 1978 World Series, the commissioner's office decided to form a study group which would come up with recommendations on how to improve umpiring.

Two weeks later, at the association's annual meeting, Luciano turned it around and announced the umpires would also form a study group but with one big difference: they would investigate ways and means of improving the commissioner's office and the offices of the league presidents. There are fifty-two members of the association. When Luciano asked for a show of hands as to which umpires would be willing to serve on this committee he counted fifty-three hands.

For a while it seemed just about everyone had a chance to rate the umpires. The general managers of all twenty-six clubs still submit annual rankings. Until a few years ago the players also rated us. It was ridiculous. An umpire calls a player out on a tough play and often the player insists he's the victim of bad umpiring. They're prejudiced in their own behalf. So are the general managers. They're like the field managers. They see the game one way. In the late 1960s, for example, the San Francisco Giants were angry over a call made by Harry Wendelstedt. Like an elephant, the Giants didn't forget. For the next six years they gave Wendelstedt a low rating. The only ones who should rate us are our supervisors, Al Barlick of the National League and Dick Butler of the American League.

The retirement age for umpires is fifty-five, but it isn't always enforced. A few umpires have been allowed to work beyond fifty-five. I was among the lucky ones. I didn't retire until I was fifty-seven, after I had twenty-five years in the league. Not many umpires have that long a career.

The toughest thing was telling the kids. They couldn't understand it. They thought their father would go on forever. But it doesn't work that way. The official announcement was made on September 26, 1976, at Shea Stadium, the home of the New York Mets. It was an appropriate place for me to begin saying good-bye. I had been lucky enough to work the plate in the first game played at Shea Stadium.

In the seventh or eighth inning, my retirement was announced on the message board and I got a big send-off. After the game, when I was walking off the field, Commissioner Bowie Kuhn came over and said, "Tom, I'm very surprised to see a man like you retire."

I said, "Well, it wasn't my idea. It was Chub's."

And the commissioner said, "That's not right. We need umpires like you around, with experience, who can do the job."

In the runway, Donald Grant, the president of the Mets, asked me if I would come upstairs. "We're having a little party for you," he said. He told me to bring my kids. All the ballplayers and newspapermen were there and they toasted me with champagne, and everybody came over and congratulated me and wished me luck.

The next day we went down to Philadelphia for the final series of the season. That was the end of the line. On Saturday night, the second game of the series, I had the plate, my last plate game. My retirement was announced in the eighth inning. There were forty thousand people in the stands and they actually stopped the game. And this was in Philadelphia, the toughest park in the league. The ballplayers came out of both dugouts and waved and applauded, and the fans responded with more cheers. I turned around, with my back toward the field, and took a bow.

I got all choked up. It was a special thing to happen to an umpire. And it was nice for my kids. My daughter and my three sons were there. And I thought of my wife, Margie, and the day many years before, when she said, "Tom, why don't you give it a try."

Bob Boone, who was catching for the Phillies, turned around and said, "Tom, it's been a pleasure to work in front of you. You've been a great umpire all these years. If all the umpires were like you there wouldn't be so much trouble. I can't understand why some of them carry a chip on their shoulder."

"Bob," I said, "umpires don't carry chips."

Then he wished me luck and told me his father, who had also been a major-league ballplayer, always had a lot of respect for me. I was surprised and pleased.

Everybody came over to me after the game. The groundskeepers, the security men, the ushers. Even Ruly Carpenter, the young fellow who owns the Phillies, patted me on the back and wished me luck. So did Danny Ozark, the Philadelphia manager.

Now Tug McGraw, the Phillies' relief pitcher, is no angel. But he followed me up the runway and gave me a hug. Ron Reed, another relief pitcher, shook my hand and said, "It's been a pleasure. Every time I was on the mound and you had the plate, I knew I was going to get a fair shot."

They had champagne for me in the Phillies' dressing room. Bill Giles, Warren's son, who is an executive with the Phillies, had ordered the champagne and then, lo and behold, in walked Mr. Giles. He was in his eighties and not in the best of health. When he came in he had tears in his eyes and that brought tears to my eyes.

The hardest thing was saying good-bye to my partners the next day. I looked at John McSherry and he looked at me. We couldn't say anything. Terry Tata wished me luck. Then Billy Williams came to say good-bye. Not good-bye, actually—just so long. But we knew we'd never be working together again.

An elderly lady stopped me on my way out of the ball park. I had never seen her before and haven't seen her since.

"Mr. Gorman," she said.

"Yes, ma'am."

"Would you please sign my program? I've been watching you as long as I've known baseball."

I signed her program and she handed me a cake. "Mr. Gorman, would you please take this," she said.

I wish I had that lady's name or address. It's the best cake I ever ate. And it made me feel that maybe, after all, umpires are not only needed, but appreciated.

I was the last of the old gang to get out. We had some great umpires—Jocko Conlan and Al Barlick and Babe Pinelli, Dusty Boggess, Frank Secory, Frank Dascoli, Lou Jorda, and Artie Gore. The game of baseball doesn't change but there is a constant evolution, new people coming in and older guys like myself going out.

The first year out was tough for me. But I was lucky because over the years, during the off-season, I had been representing the Old Grand-Dad Division of National Distillers, touring the country making speeches in their behalf. And when I retired they put me on full time. But busy as I was, I missed umpiring. Whenever I saw a sandlot game, I'd stop and get out of the car and watch an inning or two. And I was always aware that, win or lose, the players were having a good time. Once, in Newark, New Jersey, a few miles from where I live, there was a rhubarb on a play at the plate and the fellow who was umpiring quit and took off. I was tempted to introduce myself, and say, "Fellows, I'm Tom Gorman, worked in the National League for twenty-five years. I'll work a few innings for you." But I didn't say anything. I got back in the car and drove home.

Two weeks later I got a call from Fred Fleig and he asked if I could take the next flight to Cincinnati and fill in for a few games. Satch Davidson had been hit in the ribs by a pitch. Later, Harry Wendelstedt got hurt and then Ed Vargo was out with a bad hand, and so I kept working. Chub Feeney had kept me on the payroll as sort of a combination promotion–public relations man. I'd make a few speeches, and work two or three exhibitions, the Hall of Fame game in Cooperstown, New York, and the Mayor's Trophy game between the Yankees and the Mets. Later, I represented Commissioner Kuhn at the Babe Ruth World Series and the American Legion tournament.

Sometimes the telephone doesn't ring and you get to feeling sorry for yourself. You think you've been forgotten. But then I'd get a call from one of the clubs asking if I'd like to appear at their Old-Timers' game, and I'm off again. George Steinbrenner, who owns the Yankees, called two years in a row to ask if I had World Series tickets. Chub Feeney called, too. He offered me tickets, but that wasn't really why he called. He knows I can always come up with a few tickets. It was Chub's way of telling me I hadn't been forgotten.

I saw Frank Sinatra at the 1978 World Series. Sinatra's been a good friend of Leo Durocher for many years. We talked about the fact that Leo doesn't go out much anymore. Frank gave me Leo's number. I was thinking maybe I'd give him a call and buck him up a little.

Index